200 Verbs 2,000 Sentences
Latin American Spanish
Frequency List

200 Verbs 2,000 Sentences
Latin American Spanish
Frequency List

ISBN: 978-1-952161-13-1

www.L2Press.com

First Edition

This Spanish book series is dedicated to

Alexander Argüelles, Luca Lampariello, and Mikel Telleria Mujika

for their practical contributions to self-taught language learners.

Thank you.

Introduction

This book introduces the 200 most frequent Spanish verbs, which account for about 90% of the verbs you'll encounter in everyday conversation and writing. Each verb is presented through 10 simple example sentences that highlight a variety of the most commonly used tenses and conjugations. But you're not just learning verbs in isolation. Each verb appears alongside the words it frequently pairs with, including common nouns, adjectives, adverbs, and prepositions that native speakers use all the time. As a result, you'll repeatedly see and absorb the vocabulary that most often appears with these high-frequency verbs. Over the course of the book, this adds up to exposure to thousands of useful words and patterns. Think of this book not just as a guide to 200 verbs, but as a gateway to the core vocabulary and patterns that shape natural, everyday Spanish.

The beauty of this method lies in its simplicity. Short, easy-to-understand sentences allow you to focus on building a solid foundation without feeling overwhelmed. Experienced language learners tend to make faster progress when they're exposed to large amounts of clear, understandable language rather than focusing heavily on grammar rules. With that in mind, you'll learn primarily through meaningful repetition and practical examples while developing the ability to infer meaning from context, one of the most valuable skills for long-term proficiency and fluency. By encountering words and structures repeatedly in various meaningful contexts, you'll gradually develop an intuitive feel for Spanish that goes beyond memorization.

By the time you complete this book and its companions, "200 Nouns" and "200 Adjectives", you'll have built a vocabulary and intuition strong enough to dive into authentic content made for native Spanish speakers. While this book introduces many common nouns and adjectives in context, the companion books give them the dedicated, systematic treatment they deserve, ensuring the highest-frequency words in each category are fully covered, not just encountered in passing. Together, these three books cover the highest-frequency words across the most essential categories of Spanish, giving you a solid, well-rounded foundation.

The Spanish in this book reflects Latin American usage, with a slight emphasis on Mexico. The audio is read by a native Mexican speaker, so you'll hear a clear, neutral Mexican accent throughout. The vocabulary is easily understood across Latin America (and even Spain), while staying grounded in everyday Mexican usage. Mexico is home to more Spanish speakers than any other country, making its variety of Spanish an ideal foundation for anyone learning the language.

Audio is where everything comes together. Reading helps you recognize patterns, but listening and speaking is what turns those patterns into real, usable language. When you hear the sentences spoken clearly and naturally, you begin to internalize pronunciation, rhythm, and flow. Your Spanish will start to feel more automatic and authentic. The complete audio for this book allows you to reinforce every sentence through repeated exposure, helping you connect what you see on the page with how it actually sounds. You can listen while reading, repeat aloud while reading, or listen on its own to train your ear. This kind of consistent repetition is the fastest way to build real fluency. If you want to move beyond recognizing Spanish to truly understanding and using it, combining the book with the audio is essential. The full audio of this book is available for purchase at L2Press.com.

Ready to start your Spanish journey the smart and efficient way? This book offers you a clear path to success. Whether your goal is to connect with Spanish-speaking friends, enhance your career opportunities, or immerse yourself in the rich culture of Mexico, Colombia, and other Spanish-speaking countries, this book will get you there faster and more effectively than traditional grammar-based approaches. Don't waste time on inefficient learning methods. Begin your transformation into a confident Spanish speaker today with this focused and practical approach to language learning.

How to use this book

Build Spanish fluency by rotating through three powerful techniques: shadowing, reading aloud, active recall:

- Shadowing is a form of active listening. Listen to the audio and repeat it aloud nearly simultaneously, following the speaker like a shadow. You can do this while reading the Spanish, the English, or without looking at the text. Focus on sounding like the native speaker. Pay attention to vowel sounds, vowel length, new consonant sounds, stress, and intonation.
- Reading aloud bridges the gap between written and spoken Spanish. Simply read the sentences out loud at your own pace. This helps you build confidence, improve pronunciation, and get used to hearing your own voice in Spanish.
- Active recall here means translating from English into Spanish. Cover the Spanish and try to produce the Spanish you've been practicing. It's the most effective and challenging step, as it forces your brain to retrieve the language instead of just recognizing it.

Note that you speak aloud in each step. This is critical for training your mouth and tongue. Language is a physical skill as much as a mental one, and your ability to understand and recall Spanish will only take you so far if your mouth isn't trained to produce it. Whether you are shadowing, reading aloud, or doing active recall, speaking in every step builds the muscle memory needed to form sounds quickly, smoothly, and naturally. This repeated, active production is what turns passive knowledge into real speaking ability.

These three techniques work together as a single learning loop that you repeat with the same material. Rather than moving on to new material each day, you return to the same sentences in different ways. You begin by hearing and imitating the language through shadowing, which builds familiarity with the sounds and rhythm. Then you reinforce that familiarity by reading aloud at your own pace, giving your brain more time to process and your mouth more time to practice. Finally, you test and strengthen what you've learned through active recall, forcing yourself to produce the language on your own. Each step prepares you for the next, and each pass through the loop deepens your understanding and ability. Over time, what once felt unfamiliar will become more automatic.

I recommend spending about 30 minutes per day with this book. On the first day, shadow six pages. On the second day, go back to those same six pages and read them aloud at your own pace. On the third day, cover the Spanish and try to actively recall the sentences by translating from English. If you can produce at least half of them with reasonable accuracy, that's a good sign you're ready to move on to the next set of pages. If not, simply repeat the cycle. There's no need to rush. Going back over the same material is not a setback. It's how you learn. Some sections will click quickly, while others may take an extra pass or two. The goal is steady progress and growing familiarity, not perfection.

Your goal is not to memorize every sentence in this book. Your goal is exposure. By working through many examples of the most common verbs and structures, you start to recognize patterns without having to think about them. You'll encounter the same words and constructions multiple times in slightly different contexts, and your brain will absorb them naturally over time. Some sentences will stick and others won't, and that's perfectly fine. What matters is building a deep familiarity with how Spanish works. That familiarity is what allows you to understand real Spanish and respond with confidence.

Recommended routine

A 3-day loop that will produce excellent results (Day 1 - Shadow, Day 2 - Read aloud, Day 3 - Active recall):

Day 1 of pages 1-6	Shadow Spanish twice (first while looking at Spanish & then while looking at English)
Day 2 of pages 1-6	Read Spanish aloud, look at English translation, read Spanish aloud again
Day 3 of pages 1-6	Active recall (cover the Spanish and translate the English into Spanish aloud)
Day 1 of pages 7-12	Shadow Spanish twice (first while looking at Spanish & then while looking at English)
Day 2 of pages 7-12	Read Spanish aloud, look at English translation, read Spanish aloud again
Day 3 of pages 7-12	Active recall (cover the Spanish and translate the English into Spanish aloud)
Day 1 of pages 13-18	Shadow Spanish twice (first while looking at Spanish & then while looking at English)
Day 2 of pages 13-18	Read Spanish aloud, look at English translation, read Spanish aloud again
Day 3 of pages 13-18	Active recall (cover the Spanish and translate the English into Spanish aloud)
Day 1 of pages 19-24	Shadow Spanish twice (first while looking at Spanish & then while looking at English)
Day 2 of pages 19-24	Read Spanish aloud, look at English translation, read Spanish aloud again
Day 3 of pages 19-24	Active recall (cover the Spanish and translate the English into Spanish aloud)
Day 1 of pages 25-30	Shadow Spanish twice (first while looking at Spanish & then while looking at English)
Day 2 of pages 25-30	Read Spanish aloud, look at English translation, read Spanish aloud again
Day 3 of pages 25-30	Active recall (cover the Spanish and translate the English into Spanish aloud)
Day 1 of pages 31-36	Shadow Spanish twice (first while looking at Spanish & then while looking at English)
Day 2 of pages 31-36	Read Spanish aloud, look at English translation, read Spanish aloud again
Day 3 of pages 31-36	Active recall (cover the Spanish and translate the English into Spanish aloud)
Day 1 of pages 37-42	Shadow Spanish twice (first while looking at Spanish & then while looking at English)
Day 2 of pages 37-42	Read Spanish aloud, look at English translation, read Spanish aloud again
Day 3 of pages 37-42	Active recall (cover the Spanish and translate the English into Spanish aloud)
Day 1 of pages 43-48	Shadow Spanish twice (first while looking at Spanish & then while looking at English)
Day 2 of pages 43-48	Read Spanish aloud, look at English translation, read Spanish aloud again
Day 3 of pages 43-48	Active recall (cover the Spanish and translate the English into Spanish aloud)
Day 1 of pages 49-54	Shadow Spanish twice (first while looking at Spanish & then while looking at English)
Day 2 of pages 49-54	Read Spanish aloud, look at English translation, read Spanish aloud again
Day 3 of pages 49-54	Active recall (cover the Spanish and translate the English into Spanish aloud)
Day 1 of pages 55-60	Shadow Spanish twice (first while looking at Spanish & then while looking at English)
Day 2 of pages 55-60	Read Spanish aloud, look at English translation, read Spanish aloud again
Day 3 of pages 55-60	Active recall (cover the Spanish and translate the English into Spanish aloud)
Day 1 of pages 61-67	Shadow Spanish twice (first while looking at Spanish & then while looking at English)
Day 2 of pages 61-67	Read Spanish aloud, look at English translation, read Spanish aloud again
Day 3 of pages 61-67	Active recall (cover the Spanish and translate the English into Spanish aloud)

What to do after this book series

This book series gives you a strong, intermediate-level foundation in Spanish. Once you finish it, the next step is to move into real-world Spanish, where your progress will come from continued exposure, active use, and consistent practice. Here are some of the most effective ways to keep improving with native materials.

Reading: There are two main methods language learners use to read, intensive reading and extensive reading. Intensive reading means working through a small amount of text carefully, looking up words and paying attention to grammar and sentence structure. Extensive reading means reading quickly and fluidly for enjoyment, without stopping to look things up, to build overall exposure to the language. Do both. Read books written for native speakers, starting with simpler ones, and consider reading Spanish versions of books you've already read and know well. Choose topics and genres you enjoy. Over time, extensive reading builds familiarity with vocabulary and structure, while intensive reading helps you understand the details more deeply. Don't forget to read aloud some of the time.

Watching and Listening: Watch TV shows, movies, and listen to podcasts in Spanish on topics you already enjoy. In the beginning, look for simpler native content. Then gradually move on to more advanced content, even if you don't catch everything. To get the most out of any episode, read a transcript beforehand to prime your brain and familiarize yourself with new words and phrases. Then watch or listen attentively and review the transcript afterward. Repeat this process as often as you like, while also exposing yourself to a wide variety of content. Over time, your ear will adapt, your vocabulary will grow, and what once felt confusing will start to feel natural.

Speaking: Find a native speaker and converse with them on a consistent basis. The ideal practice partner is patient and will not simply correct your errors but will prompt you to self-correct and express your ideas more clearly. If you want to speak fluently, there is no substitute for regular conversation. Try to schedule consistent sessions, even if they are short, and focus on communicating your thoughts rather than speaking perfectly. Mistakes are part of the process. Prepare a few topics or questions beforehand to keep the conversation flowing, and reuse phrases you've learned so they become automatic. You will eventually notice that what once required effort starts to come naturally, and your confidence will grow with each interaction.

Language Islands: A language island is a personal collection of sentences built around specific situations in your own life, practiced until they become automatic so the language is already there when you need it. The idea is to build small islands of fluency around moments you're likely to find yourself in, such as introducing yourself, ordering food, talking about your work or your family. To create one, write about 20 simple, natural sentences you would actually say in that situation, then practice them out loud until they feel effortless. Eventually you can expand their complexity by adding details, changing verb tenses, and swapping vocabulary. Over time, your islands grow and connect, and your speech becomes faster, more natural, and more confident.

Travel and Immersion: Visit a Spanish-speaking country and avoid using any language but Spanish. When you're immersed, every interaction becomes a lesson. The pressure of real communication accelerates your progress in a way that structured study simply cannot. You will make mistakes and occasionally feel lost, but that discomfort is exactly what helps the language to click. Even short trips can lead to noticeable progress if you fully commit to using Spanish.

1 – ser	**to be (permanent characteristics)**
¿De dónde eres?	Where are you from?
Soy de Buenos Aires.	I'm from Buenos Aires.
Ella es alta.	She is tall.
El hielo es frío.	Ice is cold.
Son las tres de la tarde.	It's three in the afternoon.
Cuando yo era niño, era muy tímido.	When I was a child, I was very shy.
Fui el primero en llegar.	I was the first to arrive.
Siempre he sido una persona puntual.	I have always been a punctual person.
La conferencia será en el auditorio principal.	The conference will be in the main auditorium.
Quiero ser médico cuando sea grande.	I want to be a doctor when I am older.

2 – estar	**to be (temporary conditions)**
¿Dónde estás?	Where are you?
Estoy en casa.	I'm at home.
¿Cómo estás?	How are you?
Estoy bien, gracias.	I'm fine, thank you.
¿Dónde está el baño?	Where is the bathroom?
Estuve en Madrid el año pasado.	I was in Madrid last year.
El paquete estará aquí el viernes.	The package will be here on Friday.
Yo estaba durmiendo cuando llamaste.	I was sleeping when you called.
Tengo que estar en casa antes de las ocho.	I have to be home before 8 o'clock.
Los niños están jugando afuera.	The kids are playing outside.

3 – tener	**to have**
Tengo hambre.	I'm hungry.
¿Cuántos años tienes?	How old are you?
Mi hermana tiene tres hijos pequeños.	My sister has three young children.
No tenemos tiempo para hacerlo ahora.	We don't have time to do it now.
Ayer tuve una reunión muy importante en el trabajo.	Yesterday I had a very important meeting at work.
Mis padres tuvieron que vender la casa el año pasado.	My parents had to sell the house last year.
He tenido un día muy ocupado en la oficina.	I've had a very busy day at the office.
¡Ten cuidado!	Be careful!
Mañana tendremos una reunión con el jefe.	Tomorrow we'll have a meeting with the boss.
Es importante tener paciencia con los niños pequeños.	It's important to have patience with small children.

4 – hacer — **to do, make**

Me hace feliz estar aquí. — It makes me happy to be here.
¿Qué haces en tu tiempo libre? — What do you do in your free time?
Hace calor. / Hace frío. — It's hot. / It's cold.
¿Qué estás haciendo? — What are you doing?
¿Por qué hiciste eso? — Why did you do that?
Hicieron un gran esfuerzo para llegar a tiempo. — They made a great effort to arrive on time.
No hagas ruido, el bebé está durmiendo. — Don't make noise, the baby is sleeping.
Haz lo que quieras. — Do whatever you want.
Voy al gimnasio a hacer ejercicio. — I'm going to the gym to exercise.
¿Puedes hacerme un favor? — Can you do me a favor?

5 – poder — **to be able to, can**

No puedo más. — I can't take it anymore.
¿Puedes ayudarme? — Can you help me?
Mi abuela ya no puede caminar muy bien. — My grandmother can't walk very well anymore.
Podemos intentarlo otra vez. — We can try again.
No pude dormir. — I couldn't sleep.
¿Pudiste resolverlo? — Were you able to solve it?
No pudimos ir. — We couldn't go.
¿Has podido contactar con María? — Have you been able to contact María?
No podíamos entender lo que el guía estaba diciendo. — We couldn't understand what the guide was saying.
Podrás hacerlo si practicas. — You'll be able to do it if you practice.

6 – decir — **to say, tell**

¿Qué dijiste? — What did you say?
Te estoy diciendo la verdad. — I'm telling you the truth.
Dicen que va a llover. — They say it's going to rain.
¿Cómo se dice ... en español? — How do you say ... in Spanish?
Te lo dije. — I told you so.
Él dijo que estaba cansado. — He said he was tired.
Diré mi opinión en la reunión. — I will say my opinion in the meeting.
¿Dirías lo mismo si estuvieras en mi lugar? — Would you say the same if you were in my place?
He dicho mil veces que no. — I have said no a thousand times.
¿Qué quieres decir con eso? — What do you mean by that?

7 – ir	**to go, leave**
Voy a casa.	I'm going home.
Me voy.	I'm leaving.
Mis hijos van al colegio a pie.	My kids go to school on foot.
¿Te vas a quedar o te vas?	Are you going to stay or leave?
No te vayas.	Don't go.
Ella se fue sin decir nada.	She left without saying anything.
Se fueron temprano.	They left early.
Iban muy rápido por la carretera.	They were going very fast on the highway.
¿Quieres ir conmigo?	Do you want to go with me?
No quiero irme todavía.	I don't want to leave yet.

8 – querer	**to want**
No quiero hablar de eso ahora.	I don't want to talk about that right now.
¿Qué quieres comer?	What do you want to eat?
Mi hijo quiere un perro para su cumpleaños.	My son wants a dog for his birthday.
Quería ayudarte, pero no supe cómo.	I wanted to help you, but I didn't know how.
Ellos no quisieron esperar más.	They didn't want to wait any longer.
Yo siempre quise ser médico cuando era niño.	I always wanted to be a doctor when I was a kid.
¿Alguna vez has querido vivir en otro país?	Have you ever wanted to live in another country?
He querido decirte esto desde hace tiempo.	I've wanted to tell you this for a while.
Querrás verlo con tus propios ojos.	You'll want to see it with your own eyes.
Se me cayó el vaso sin querer.	I accidentally dropped the glass.

9 – haber	**to have (auxiliary verb), be (there is/are)**
Hay mucho tráfico.	There is a lot of traffic.
Hay mucha gente aquí.	There are many people here.
Durante las vacaciones, no había nadie en casa.	During the vacation, no one was at home.
El lunes hubo una reunión.	On Monday there was a meeting.
Habrá una reunión mañana por la mañana.	There will be a meeting tomorrow morning.
Nunca he estado en Costa Rica.	I've never been to Costa Rica.
¿Has visto esa película?	Have you seen that movie?
Ha llegado el momento de decidir.	The moment to decide has arrived.
Hemos terminado el trabajo.	We've finished the work.
Han sido muy amables conmigo.	They have been very kind to me.

10 – ver	**to see, watch**
No veo bien sin mis lentes.	I don't see well without my glasses.
Mis hijos ven caricaturas los fines de semana.	My kids watch cartoons on weekends.
Ayer vi una película buenísima en Netflix.	Yesterday I watched a great movie on Netflix.
¿Viste el juego anoche?	Did you see the game last night?
¿Cuántas veces has visto esa película?	How many times have you seen that movie?
No te he visto desde hace meses.	I haven't seen you in months.
Hemos visto muchos cambios en los últimos años.	We've seen a lot of changes in the last few years.
Ya veremos qué pasa.	We'll see what happens.
Ya verás que todo va a salir bien.	You'll see everything's going to turn out fine.
A ver, ¿qué pasó aquí?	Let's see, what happened here?

11 – dar	**to give**
Te doy mi palabra.	I give you my word.
Él siempre me da buenos consejos.	He always gives me good advice.
Esa película me da miedo.	That movie scares me.
Le di el libro ayer.	I gave him the book yesterday.
Me di cuenta de mi error.	I realized my mistake.
Nos dieron una oportunidad.	They gave us an opportunity.
Mi hermana dio a luz ayer.	My sister gave birth yesterday.
Te daré mi respuesta mañana.	I will give you my answer tomorrow.
¿Le diste las gracias?	Did you thank him?
¿Le puedes dar esto a tu hermano?	Can you give this to your brother?

12 – saber	**to know**
No sé.	I don't know.
Sé manejar, pero no tengo carro.	I know how to drive but I don't have a car.
¿Sabes qué? Mejor nos vamos.	You know what? We better go.
Sabemos que no fue tu culpa.	We know it wasn't your fault.
Quién sabe.	Who knows.
Yo no sabía que tenías hijos.	I didn't know you had kids.
Cuando lo supimos, ya era demasiado tarde.	When we found out, it was already too late.
Pronto sabrás la verdad.	Soon you'll know the truth.
Quiero saber cuánto cuesta ese carro.	I want to know how much that car costs.
Me gustaría saber qué piensa él realmente.	I'd like to know what he really thinks.

13 – llegar | **to arrive**
¿A qué hora llegas? | What time are you arriving?
Llego a casa a las seis. | I get home at six.
¿A qué hora llega el tren? | What time does the train arrive?
Mis padres llegan mañana. | My parents arrive tomorrow.
¿Ya llegó el paquete? | Did the package arrive yet?
Llegaron juntos. | They arrived together.
Cuando llegue el momento, sabrás qué hacer. | When the time comes, you'll know what to do.
Llegó la hora de decir la verdad. | The time has come to tell the truth.
Acabo de llegar. | I just got here.
Voy a llegar un poco más tarde hoy. | I'm going to arrive a bit later today.

14 – pasar | **to happen, pass, spend (time)**
Los domingos paso tiempo con mi familia. | On Sundays I spend time with my family.
El autobús pasa por aquí cada media hora. | The bus passes by here every half hour.
¿Qué pasa? | What's up?
Pasé tres años viviendo en Madrid. | I spent three years living in Madrid.
¿Qué pasó en la reunión de ayer? | What happened at yesterday's meeting?
No pasó nada grave. | Nothing serious happened.
Pasamos todo el día en la playa. | We spent the whole day at the beach.
Pasaré toda la semana preparando el examen. | I will spend the whole week preparing for the exam.
¿Qué pasará si no llegamos a tiempo? | What will happen if we don't arrive on time?
Voy a pasar el día en casa de mis abuelos. | I'm going to spend the day at my grandparents' house.

15 – poner | **to put, become, set**
¿Dónde pongo esto? | Where do I put this?
Me pongo roja cuando me da vergüenza. | I turn red when I'm embarrassed.
Ella se pone nerviosa cuando habla en público. | She gets nervous when she speaks in public.
El sol se pone a las ocho. | The sun sets at eight.
No pongas tus pies en el sofá. | Don't put your feet on the sofa.
Me puse el abrigo porque hacía frío. | I put on my coat because it was cold.
Nos pusimos muy contentos al ver a nuestros abuelos. | We got very happy when we saw our grandparents.
Ya hemos puesto las luces de Navidad. | We've already put up the Christmas lights.
¿Puedes ponerle gasolina al carro? | Can you put gas in the car?
¿Puedes poner la mesa, por favor? | Can you set the table, please?

16 – hablar | **to speak, talk**

Solo hablo inglés, pero estoy aprendiendo español. | I speak only English, but I'm learning Spanish.
Ella habla tres idiomas. | She speaks three languages.
Ella habla muy rápido y no entiendo nada. | She speaks very fast, and I don't understand anything.
¿Con quién estás hablando? | Who are you talking to?
¿Has hablado con él últimamente? | Have you talked to him lately?
Hablamos ayer después del trabajo. | We spoke yesterday after work.
Hablando de trabajo, ¿cómo va tu nuevo empleo? | Speaking of work, how's your new job going?
Mientras estés en esta casa, solo hablarás español. | While you're in this house, you'll speak only Spanish.
Los bebés empiezan a hablar alrededor del primer año. | Babies start to talk around their first year.
¿Puedes hablar más despacio? | Can you speak more slowly?

17 – creer | **to believe**

¿Me crees? | Do you believe me?
Te creo. | I believe you.
¿Crees en Dios? | Do you believe in God?
Ella no cree en fantasmas. | She doesn't believe in ghosts.
Creemos en la importancia de la educación. | We believe in the importance of education.
Siempre he creído en ti. | I've always believed in you.
Creemos que es la mejor decisión. | We believe it's the best decision.
Si no crees en ti mismo, nadie lo hará. | If you don't believe in yourself, no one will.
Han creído en nuestro proyecto desde el principio. | They have believed in our project from the beginning.
¿Me creerías si te lo contara? | Would you believe me if I told you?

18 – deber | **to owe, should, must**

Debo hacer mi tarea antes de jugar. | I have to do my homework before playing.
No debes manejar si bebiste alcohol. | You should not drive if you drank alcohol.
Los estudiantes deben respetar las normas escolares. | Students must respect the school rules.
Debí haber llegado antes. | I should have arrived earlier.
Deberías llamar a tus padres más seguido. | You should call your parents more often.
Deberíamos comer más sano. | We should eat healthier.
Debemos salir ya si queremos llegar a tiempo. | We must leave now if we want to be on time.
No debiste decir eso. | You shouldn't have said that.
¿Cuánto me debes? | How much do you owe me?
Te debo cincuenta pesos. | I owe you fifty pesos.

19 – dejar	**to leave, let, stop**
¿Puedo dejar esto aquí?	Can I leave this here?
¿Me dejas entrar?	Will you let me in?
Déjame en paz.	Leave me alone.
Mis padres no me dejan salir esta noche.	My parents won't let me go out tonight.
Dejé de fumar hace dos años.	I quit smoking two years ago.
Mi madre me dejó dinero para comprar comida.	My mother left me money to buy food.
Juan dejó un mensaje para ti.	Juan left a message for you.
No dejes la puerta abierta.	Don't leave the door open.
Dejamos a los niños con mis padres.	We left the kids with my parents.
¿Puedes dejar de gritar?	Can you stop shouting?

20 – parecer	**to seem, appear, look like**
Parece que va a llover más tarde.	It looks like it's going to rain later.
Me parece una buena idea.	I think it's a good idea.
Tu hermana se parece mucho a tu mamá.	Your sister looks a lot like your mom.
Este restaurante parece muy bueno.	This restaurant looks very good.
Pareces preocupado, ¿todo bien?	You seem worried, is everything okay?
Los gemelos parecen iguales, no los distingo.	The twins look the same, I can't tell them apart.
Al principio parecía difícil, pero ya me acostumbré.	At first it seemed hard, but I've gotten used to it.
Ese castigo nunca me ha parecido justo.	That punishment has never seemed fair to me.
Parecían contentos con los resultados.	They seemed happy with the results.
Parecía que iba a nevar, pero no.	It seemed like it was going to snow, but it didn't.

21 – seguir	**to keep doing something, follow**
Sigo sin entender lo que pasó.	I still don't understand what happened.
¿Sigues trabajando en la misma empresa?	Are you still working at the same company?
Mi perro me sigue a todos lados.	My dog follows me everywhere.
Sígueme, te voy a mostrar algo.	Follow me, I'm going to show you something.
Sigue tus sueños, no escuches a nadie.	Follow your dreams, don't listen to anyone.
Sigue caminando, ya casi llegamos.	Keep walking, we're almost there.
Ella siguió hablando como si nada hubiera pasado.	She kept talking as if nothing had happened.
He seguido todos los pasos del tutorial.	I've followed all the steps in the tutorial.
Si todo va bien, seguiré aquí el próximo año.	If everything goes well, I'll stay here next year.
Necesito seguir adelante con mis planes.	I need to move forward with my plans.

22 – quedar(se)	**to remain, stay, be left**
Me quedo en casa.	I'm staying home.
¿Dónde queda el banco?	Where is the bank located?
Solo quedan dos boletos para el concierto.	Only two tickets are left for the concert.
Me queda una semana de vacaciones.	I have one week of vacation left.
Nos estamos quedando en el cuarto piso del hotel.	We're staying on the fourth floor of the hotel.
Él se quedó callado.	He stayed quiet.
Me quedaría contigo si no tuviera que trabajar.	I would stay with you if I didn't have to work.
Me quedaré aquí hasta que llegues.	I will stay here until you arrive.
Quédate aquí mientras voy por el carro.	Stay here while I go get the car.
Prefiero quedarme en casa que salir con esta lluvia.	I prefer to stay home rather than go out in this rain.

23 – llevar	**to carry, take, wear**
Llevo a los niños al colegio todas las mañanas.	I take the kids to school every morning.
Te llevo al aeropuerto.	I'll take you to the airport.
¿Qué llevas puesto?	What are you wearing?
Llevo una camisa azul.	I'm wearing a blue shirt.
Ella lleva un vestido rojo muy bonito.	She's wearing a very pretty red dress.
Llevo dos años estudiando español.	I've been studying Spanish for two years.
No llevo dinero.	I'm not carrying any money.
No me llevo bien con mi jefe.	I don't get along well with my boss.
Llevé a mi perro al veterinario.	I took my dog to the vet.
¿Puedes llevar esto por mí, por favor?	Can you carry this for me, please?

24 – encontrar	**to find**
No encuentro mi celular por ningún lado.	I can't find my cell phone anywhere.
Encontré las llaves debajo del sofá.	I found the keys under the sofa.
¿Dónde encontraste ese libro?	Where did you find that book?
¿Has encontrado tu teléfono?	Have you found your phone?
Encontré dinero en la calle.	I found money on the street.
Finalmente encontré un estacionamiento.	I finally found a parking spot.
Encontramos un restaurante increíble en esa calle.	We found an amazing restaurant on that street.
¿Cómo te encuentras hoy?	How are you feeling today?
Me encontré con un viejo amigo en el supermercado.	I ran into an old friend at the supermarket.
No puedo encontrar mis llaves.	I can't find my keys.

25 – pensar — **to think**

Pienso que tienes razón. — I think you're right.
A veces pienso en cómo era todo antes. — Sometimes I think about how everything used to be.
¿En qué piensas? — What are you thinking about?
Mi mamá piensa que trabajo demasiado. — My mom thinks I work too much.
No pensé que fuera tan caro. — I didn't think it would be that expensive.
Nunca pensé que esto me pasaría. — I never thought this would happen to me.
Estaba pensando en llamarte más tarde. — I was thinking about calling you later.
De niño, pensaba que los adultos sabían todo. — As a kid, I thought adults knew everything.
Pensábamos que llovería, pero salió el sol. — We thought it would rain, but the sun came out.
Voy a pensarlo bien antes de decidir. — I'm going to think it over carefully before deciding.

26 – volver — **to return, come back, become**

Ahorita vuelvo, voy al baño. — I'll be right back, I'm going to the bathroom.
¿A qué hora vuelves a casa? — What time do you get back home?
Los niños vuelven del colegio a las tres. — The children return from school at three.
Volví al restaurante donde comimos la semana pasada. — I went back to the restaurant we ate at last week.
Nunca volví a ver a esa persona. — I never saw that person again.
María volvió de vacaciones el lunes pasado. — María returned from vacation last Monday.
Él se volvió loco cuando escuchó la noticia. — He went crazy when he heard the news.
Mi abuela se ha vuelto muy olvidadiza. — My grandma has become very forgetful.
Te prometo que volveré temprano. — I promise you I'll come back early.
No quiero volver a ese lugar. — I don't want to go back to that place.

27 – salir — **to go out, leave**

¿A qué hora sales del trabajo normalmente? — What time do you normally leave work?
Salgo de la oficina a las cinco. — I leave the office at five.
Mis hijos salen con sus amigos los fines de semana. — My kids go out with their friends on the weekends.
Salí temprano para evitar el tráfico. — I left early to avoid the traffic.
Todo salió mejor de lo esperado. — Everything turned out better than expected.
De joven, salía mucho los fines de semana. — When I was young, I went out a lot on weekends.
De niños, salíamos a jugar después de hacer la tarea. — As kids, we went out to play after doing homework.
Sal ya, te estoy esperando afuera. — Come out now, I'm waiting for you outside.
El nuevo modelo saldrá en diciembre. — The new model will come out in December.
Hoy no quiero salir, estoy cansado. — I don't want to go out today, I'm tired.

28 – venir | **to come**

Vengo del mercado, por eso traigo bolsas. — I'm coming from the market, that's why I have bags.
Ven acá. — Come here.
Mi primo viene de lejos para ver el juego. — My cousin comes from far away to see the game.
¿Vienes conmigo? — Are you coming with me?
¿Por qué no viniste? — Why didn't you come?
Vinimos en autobús porque el carro se dañó. — We came by bus because the car broke down.
¿Has venido antes a este restaurante? — Have you come to this restaurant before?
Siempre veníamos a esta playa en verano. — We always came to this beach in the summer.
Vendré si me da tiempo. — I'll come if I have time.
¿Vas a venir a cenar con nosotros esta noche? — Are you going to come have dinner with us tonight?

29 – llamar | **to call**

Siempre llamo a mis abuelos los domingos. — I always call my grandparents on Sundays.
¿Cómo te llamas? — What's your name?
Me llamo Daniel. — My name is Daniel.
¿Cómo se llama él? — What's his name?
¿Cómo se llama esto en español? — What is this called in Spanish?
Mi mamá y yo nos llamamos todos los días. — My mom and I call each other every day.
Llamé pero no contestaste. — I called, but you didn't answer.
Llamamos a un plomero porque había una fuga. — We called a plumber because there was a leak.
¿Me puedes llamar? — Can you call me?
¿Te puedo llamar en un rato? — Can I call you in a bit?

30 – mirar | **to look**

Miro por la ventana para ver los pájaros. — I look out the window to watch the birds.
No me mires así. — Don't look at me like that.
Ella mira su teléfono constantemente. — She looks at her phone constantly.
¡Mira lo que hice! — Look what I did!
Mira esto, lo vas a amar. — Look at this, you're going to love it.
Mira hacia ambos lados antes de cruzar. — Look both ways before crossing.
Miré por la ventana y vi que estaba lloviendo. — I looked out the window and saw that it was raining.
Ella me miró sin decir una palabra. — She looked at me without saying a word.
Mira las instrucciones si no sabes qué hacer. — Look at the instructions if you don't know what to do.
Voy a mirar el precio antes de comprar. — I'll look at the price before buying.

31 – conocer | **to know, meet**

Conozco Madrid muy bien. — I know Madrid very well.
¿Conoces a mi hermano? — Do you know my brother?
Ella no conoce la historia completa. — She doesn't know the full story.
Ellos conocen las reglas del juego. — They know the rules of the game.
Nunca conocí a mis abuelos. — I never knew my grandparents.
¿Ya conociste al nuevo profesor? — Did you already meet the new teacher?
Nos conocimos en la universidad. — We met at university.
Conocerás a mis padres mañana. — You'll meet my parents tomorrow.
No conocía a nadie en la fiesta. — I didn't know anyone at the party.
Nunca he conocido a alguien así. — I've never met someone like that.

32 – tomar | **to take, drink**

Tomo café todas las mañanas. — I drink coffee every morning.
¿Tomas café o té? — Do you drink coffee or tea?
Tomé un taxi al aeropuerto. — I took a taxi to the airport.
¿Ya te tomaste la pastilla? — Did you take your pill yet?
Tomamos unas cervezas anoche. — We drank a few beers last night.
De niño, tomaba leche con chocolate todos los días. — As a kid, I drank chocolate milk every day.
Estoy tomando un curso de fotografía. — I'm taking a photography course.
Tomaremos el vuelo de noche para ahorrar dinero. — We'll take the night flight to save money.
Tenemos que tomar una decisión pronto. — We have to make a decision soon.
¿Quieres tomar algo? — Do you want something to drink?

33 – sentir | **to feel**

Me siento cansado después del trabajo. — I feel tired after work.
Siento mucho lo que pasó. — I'm really sorry about what happened.
¿Cómo te sientes hoy? — How do you feel today?
Me sentí muy nervioso antes de la entrevista. — I felt really nervous before the interview.
¿Sintieron ustedes el temblor anoche? — Did you feel the earthquake last night?
Sentimos un temblor anoche. — We felt an earthquake last night.
Nos hemos sentido muy bienvenidos en este lugar. — We have felt very welcome in this place.
Nunca me había sentido tan feliz. — I had never felt so happy.
Me sentiré mejor después de descansar un poco. — I'll feel better after getting some rest.
Vas a sentir algo de dolor. — You're going to feel some pain.

34 – tratar | **to try, treat, be about**

Siempre trato de llegar temprano. | I always try to arrive early.
¿De qué trata esta película? | What is this movie about?
Los médicos tratan a los pacientes con mucho cuidado. | The doctors treat patients with great care.
Mis padres me tratan como si fuera un niño. | My parents treat me like I'm a child.
Lo traté bien. | I treated him well.
La película trataba sobre la guerra civil. | The movie was about the civil war.
¿Has tratado de hablar con ella? | Have you tried talking to her?
Trataré de explicarlo lo más claro posible. | I'll try to explain it as clearly as possible.
Trata de estudiar un poco cada día. | Try to study a little each day.
Voy a tratar de llegar antes de las ocho. | I'm going to try to arrive before eight.

35 – vivir | **to live**

¿Dónde vives? | Where do you live?
Vivo con mis padres todavía. | I still live with my parents.
Mis abuelos viven en un pueblito tranquilo. | My grandparents live in a quiet little town.
Viví en México por tres años cuando era joven. | I lived in Mexico for three years when I was young.
Mi abuela vivió noventa y cinco años. | My grandmother lived ninety-five years.
Vivimos momentos difíciles durante la pandemia. | We lived through difficult times during the pandemic.
Yo vivía con mis abuelos. | I used to live with my grandparents.
¿Alguna vez has vivido en otro país? | Have you ever lived in another country?
Viviré en Chile el próximo año. | I will live in Chile next year.
¿Te gustaría vivir en otro país? | Would you like to live in another country?

36 – esperar | **to wait, expect, hope**

Te espero en el carro. | I'll wait for you in the car.
Espero que estés bien. | I hope you're well.
¿Esperas algo especial para tu cumpleaños? | Do you expect something special for your birthday?
¿Estás esperando a alguien? | Are you waiting for someone?
Estoy esperando el autobús. | I'm waiting for the bus.
Te esperé por más de una hora. | I waited for you for more than an hour.
No esperaba verte aquí tan temprano. | I wasn't expecting to see you here so early.
¿Cuánto tiempo más tenemos que esperar? | How much longer do we have to wait?
No vale la pena esperar tanto. | It's not worth waiting that long.
Espera un momento, por favor. | Wait a moment, please.

37 – gustar	**to like**
¿Te gusta?	Do you like it?
Me gusta.	I like it.
No me gusta.	I don't like it.
A él le gusta coleccionar monedas antiguas.	He likes to collect old coins.
¿Te gustan las películas de terror?	Do you like horror movies?
A mis hijos les gusta jugar en el parque.	My children like to play in the park.
Nos gusta viajar.	We like to travel.
Te gustaría más este platillo si no estuviera quemado.	You'd like this dish more if it wasn't burnt.
Antes me gustaba jugar ese juego, pero ya no.	I used to like playing that game but not anymore.
¿No te gustaron los postres?	Didn't you like the desserts?

38 – contar	**to tell, count**
Te voy a contar un secreto.	I'm going to tell you a secret.
¿Me cuentas un cuento antes de dormir?	Will you tell me a bedtime story?
Ella me contó todo lo que pasó en la fiesta.	She told me everything that happened at the party.
Mis abuelos siempre cuentan historias de su juventud.	My grandparents always tell stories about their youth.
Cuéntame qué pasó en la reunión.	Tell me what happened at the meeting.
¿Ya le contaste la verdad a él?	Did you already tell him the truth?
Cuenta hasta diez cuando estés enojado.	Count to ten when you're angry.
Los niños están aprendiendo a contar hasta cien.	The children are learning to count to one hundred.
Estamos contando con su apoyo para el proyecto.	We're counting on your support for the project.
Puedes contar conmigo para lo que necesites.	You can count on me for whatever you need.

39 – trabajar	**to work**
Trabajo por mi cuenta.	I work for myself.
¿Trabajas hoy o tienes el día libre?	Are you working today or do you have the day off?
Ella trabaja desde casa la mayoría del tiempo.	She works from home most of the time.
Ayer trabajé hasta las ocho de la noche.	Yesterday I worked until eight at night.
¿Dónde trabajaste antes de venir aquí?	Where did you work before coming here?
Trabajamos juntos en ese proyecto.	We worked together on that project.
He trabajado todo el día sin parar.	I've worked all day without stopping.
Cuando vivía en México, trabajaba como mesero.	When I lived in Mexico, I worked as a waiter.
Trabajaremos en equipo para resolver este problema.	We will work as a team to solve this problem.
Tengo que trabajar mañana.	I have to work tomorrow.

40 – empezar	**to start**
¿A qué hora empieza la clase?	What time does class start?
La película empieza a las ocho.	The movie starts at eight.
Está empezando a llover.	It's starting to rain.
Los niños empiezan a entender.	The children are beginning to understand.
¿Cuándo empezaste en tu nuevo trabajo?	When did you start at your new job?
Empecé a correr hace dos meses.	I started running two months ago.
Empecé a estudiar español hace tres años.	I began studying Spanish three years ago.
La reunión empezó tarde.	The meeting started late.
El concierto empezará a las siete.	The concert will start at seven.
Vamos a empezar la película.	Let's start the movie.

41 – buscar	**to look for, search**
Buscamos un apartamento nuevo.	We are looking for a new apartment.
¿Qué es lo que buscas exactamente?	What are you looking for exactly?
Busqué tu nombre en la lista, pero no estaba.	I looked for your name on the list, but it wasn't there.
Buscarás la verdad toda tu vida.	You'll search for the truth your whole life.
Estoy buscando mis llaves.	I'm looking for my keys.
Están buscando a los responsables.	They are looking for those responsible.
Buscar empleo puede ser agotador.	Looking for work can be exhausting.
¿Has buscado en todos los cajones?	Have you looked in all the drawers?
Hemos buscado por todas partes.	We have looked everywhere.
Busca en el cajón de arriba.	Look in the top drawer.

42 – perder	**to lose, miss**
Me pierdo fácilmente sin GPS.	I get lost easily without GPS.
Mi equipo pierde casi todos los partidos.	My team loses almost every game.
Perdemos mucho tiempo en el tráfico.	We waste a lot of time in traffic.
Perdí mi celular en el parque.	I lost my phone in the park.
¿Alguna vez has perdido algo muy valioso?	Have you ever lost something really valuable?
Me perdí.	I got lost.
Te perdiste la fiesta.	You missed the party.
Marta perdió el vuelo por llegar tarde.	Marta missed the flight because she was late.
Nos perdimos en el bosque.	We got lost in the forest.
Tienes que aprender a perder sin enojarte.	You have to learn to lose without getting angry.

43 – escribir	**to write**
Escribo con la mano derecha.	I write with my right hand.
Ella escribe novelas románticas.	She writes romantic novels.
Escribo en mi diario todas las noches.	I write in my diary every night.
Los estudiantes escriben un ensayo cada semana.	The students write an essay every week.
¿Quién escribió este libro?	Who wrote this book?
El profesor escribió la tarea en la pizarra.	The teacher wrote the homework on the board.
Yo les escribía cartas a mis abuelos.	I used to write letters to my grandparents.
Escribir cartas ya no es común.	Writing letters is no longer common.
Los niños aprendieron a escribir sus nombres.	The children learned to write their names.
¿Sabes cómo escribir tu nombre en chino?	Do you know how to write your name in Chinese?

44 – entrar	**to enter, go in**
¿Puedo entrar?	Can I come in?
Cuando entres, por favor cierra la puerta.	When you come in, please close the door.
Solo los mejores entran al equipo nacional.	Only the best get onto the national team.
¿Cómo se entra a este edificio?	How does one get into this building?
El perro entró corriendo a la casa.	The dog ran into the house.
Mi hijo entró a la universidad este año.	My son got into university this year.
Su novio entró a la casa por la ventana.	Her boyfriend entered the house through the window.
Él entró en pánico al ver la serpiente.	He panicked when he saw the snake.
No puedo entrar a mi cuenta.	I can't log into my account.
Nadie puede entrar sin identificación.	No one can enter without identification.

45 – leer	**to read**
Siempre leo antes de dormir.	I always read before going to sleep.
Leo las reseñas antes de comprar algo.	I read reviews before buying something.
Ella lee rápido pero entiende bien.	She reads fast but understands well.
¿Qué estás leyendo ahora?	What are you reading now?
Estoy leyendo un libro muy interesante.	I'm reading a very interesting book.
¿Leíste todo el informe?	Did you read the entire report?
¿Has leído este libro?	Have you read this book?
Leí ese libro en dos días.	I read that book in two days.
No me gusta leer en una pantalla.	I don't like reading on a screen.
Mi hija está aprendiendo a leer.	My daughter is learning to read.

46 – recordar — **to remember, remind**

Siempre recuerdo tu cumpleaños.	I always remember your birthday.
No recuerdo dónde puse mi teléfono.	I don't remember where I put my phone.
¿Recuerdas ese verano en el lago?	Do you remember that summer at the lake?
Esta canción me recuerda mi infancia.	This song reminds me of my childhood.
De repente recordé que tenía una cita en el dentista.	Suddenly I remembered I had a dentist appointment.
No recordaste apagar las luces.	You didn't remember to turn off the lights.
Mi mamá me recordó la cita de hoy.	My mom reminded me about today's appointment.
Ella no recordaba haber dicho eso.	She didn't remember having said that.
Estoy seguro de que recordarás este día toda tu vida.	I'm sure you'll remember this day your whole life.
Es difícil recordar tantos nombres nuevos.	It's hard to remember so many new names.

47 – morir — **to die**

El protagonista muere al final de la película.	The main character dies at the end of the movie.
Me muero de hambre, ¿cuándo vamos a cenar?	I'm dying of hunger, when are we having dinner?
Casi muero del susto cuando sonó la alarma.	I nearly died of fright when the alarm went off.
Todas las plantas de mi jardín están muriendo.	All the plants in my garden are dying.
Mi abuelo murió el año pasado de un infarto.	My grandfather died last year from a heart attack.
Mi celular murió justo cuando más lo necesitaba.	My phone died right when I needed it most.
Los dinosaurios murieron hace millones de años.	Dinosaurs died millions of years ago.
Pensé que me iba a morir.	I thought I was going to die.
Prefiero morir antes que pedirle perdón.	I'd rather die than ask him for forgiveness.
Si no llueve pronto, las plantas van a morir.	If it doesn't rain soon, the plants are going to die.

48 – recibir — **to receive, get**

Siempre recibo muchos correos los lunes.	I always get a lot of emails on Mondays.
¿Recibes el periódico en casa?	Do you get the newspaper at home?
Recibí un paquete que no estaba esperando.	I received a package I wasn't expecting.
¿Recibiste el correo que te envié anoche?	Did you get the email I sent you last night?
El entrenador recibió muchos elogios.	The coach received a lot of praise.
Los jugadores recibieron una ovación del público.	The players received an ovation from the crowd.
¿Recibiste mi mensaje?	Did you get my message?
Ella ha recibido muchos elogios por su trabajo.	She's received many compliments for her work.
Mañana recibirás los resultados del examen.	You will get the test results tomorrow.
Ella acaba de recibir una beca.	She just received a scholarship.

49 – pedir — **to ask for, request, order**

Siempre pido lo mismo en este restaurante. — I always order the same thing at this restaurant.
Pido disculpas. — I apologize.
Le pedí ayuda a mi hermano con la tarea. — I asked my brother for help with the homework.
¿Qué pediste? — What did you order?
¿Por qué no le pediste ayuda al profesor? — Why didn't you ask the teacher for help?
Ella pidió permiso para irse temprano. — She asked for permission to leave early.
Ya pedimos. — We already ordered.
Vamos a pedir la cuenta pronto. — We're going to ask for the check soon.
¿Qué vas a pedir de comer? — What are you going to order to eat?
¿Te puedo pedir un favor? — Can I ask you for a favor?

50 – permitir — **to permit, allow**

No se permite fumar. — Smoking is not allowed.
¿Me permite pasar? — May I pass?
El reglamento no permite fumar en el edificio. — The regulation doesn't allow smoking in the building.
Mis padres no me permiten salir hasta muy tarde. — My parents don't let me go out too late.
El profesor nos permitió salir temprano ayer. — The teacher let us leave early yesterday.
Me permití un chocolate después del almuerzo. — I allowed myself a chocolate after lunch.
Mi jefe me permitió tomarme el día libre. — My boss allowed me to take the day off.
No le permitieron entrar al concierto sin boleto. — They didn't let him into the concert without a ticket.
Mi mamá me permitía comer dulces los domingos. — My mom would let me eat candy on Sundays.
Tenemos que permitir que todos hablen. — We have to allow everyone to speak.

51 – preguntar — **to ask**

Siempre pregunto por ti cuando veo a tu mamá. — I always ask about you when I see your mom.
Mis hijos me preguntan por qué tengo tantas canas. — My kids ask me why I have so many gray hairs.
Mi hija pregunta por qué el cielo es azul. — My daughter asks why the sky is blue.
Te pregunté si querías venir con nosotros. — I asked you if you wanted to come with us.
¿Le preguntaste a tu jefe sobre el aumento? — Did you ask your boss about the raise?
Le he preguntado muchas veces, pero no me contesta. — I've asked him many times, but he doesn't answer me.
Mi abuelo me preguntaba cómo iban las clases. — My grandpa used to ask me how my classes were going.
Te preguntarán por tu experiencia. — They will ask you about your experience.
Si no sabes, pregúntale al profesor. — If you don't know, ask the teacher.
No tengas miedo de preguntar cuando no entiendas. — Don't be afraid to ask when you don't understand.

52 – entender | **to understand**

¿Entiendes lo que estoy diciendo? | Do you understand what I'm saying?
No entiendo lo que estás diciendo. | I don't understand what you're saying.
Entiendo tu punto de vista, pero no estoy de acuerdo. | I understand your point of view, but I don't agree.
¿Entiendes las instrucciones del examen? | Do you understand the exam instructions?
Ella entiende perfectamente el español. | She understands Spanish perfectly.
Los niños entienden más de lo que creemos. | Children understand more than we think.
Ellos se entienden sin necesidad de hablar. | They understand each other without needing to speak.
¿Puedes repetirlo? No lo entendí bien. | Can you repeat that? I didn't understand it well.
¿Entendiste la explicación? | Did you understand the explanation?
Siempre me ha costado entender las matemáticas. | I've always struggled to understand math.

53 – comenzar | **to begin, start**

Comienzo mis días con una taza de café. | I begin my days with a cup of coffee.
¿Cuándo comienza la clase? | When does the class start?
La clase comienza a las ocho en punto. | The class begins at eight o'clock sharp.
Todo comenzó con una simple pregunta. | It all began with a simple question.
Comenzamos a preocuparnos cuando él no llegó. | We began to worry when he didn't arrive.
Comenzaron una nueva vida juntos. | They began a new life together.
La conferencia comenzará pronto. | The conference will begin soon.
Comenzaré la universidad en otoño. | I'll start university in the fall.
Vamos a comenzar la reunión cuando lleguen. | We are going to begin the meeting when they arrive.
Es importante comenzar el día con un buen desayuno. | It's important to begin the day with a good breakfast.

54 – crear | **to create**

Él crea música en su tiempo libre. | He creates music in his free time.
Mi hermana crea contenido digital para redes sociales. | My sister creates digital content for social media.
El chef crea platos únicos con ingredientes locales. | The chef creates unique dishes with local ingredients.
Los artistas crean obras que reflejan la sociedad. | Artists create works that reflect society.
La empresa creó un nuevo producto revolucionario. | The company created a revolutionary new product.
¿Quién creó este logo tan original? | Who created this original logo?
Este programa fue creado para ayudar a estudiantes. | This program was created to help students.
Los programadores crearon una aplicación muy útil. | The programmers created a very useful application.
Es importante crear buenos hábitos desde joven. | It's important to create good habits from a young age.
Necesitamos crear una solución para este problema. | We need to create a solution for this problem.

55 – beber

Me gusta beber té caliente en invierno.
Bebes demasiado café.
Nunca bebemos refrescos en casa.
Ellos beben cerveza los fines de semana.
No deberías beber alcohol si vas a manejar.
Bebíamos café mientras conversábamos.
Ella bebió demasiado anoche.
Bebí un vaso de leche antes de dormir.
Yo bebía té todas las tardes en Inglaterra.
Deberías beber más agua durante el día.

to drink

I like to drink hot tea in winter.
You drink too much coffee.
We never drink soda at home.
They drink beer on weekends.
You shouldn't drink alcohol if you're going to drive.
We were drinking coffee while we were talking.
She drank too much last night.
I drank a glass of milk before bed.
I used to drink tea every afternoon in England.
You should drink more water during the day.

56 – caminar

Camino todos los días.
Caminas muy rápido.
Los niños caminan juntos al colegio.
Caminamos todos los días después de cenar.
¿Por qué estás caminando tan rápido?
Ellos caminaron por la playa al atardecer.
Caminábamos sin rumbo por la ciudad.
Caminaré contigo mañana.
Camina derecho y gira a la izquierda.
Caminarían más si tuvieran tiempo.

to walk

I walk every day.
You walk very fast.
The children walk together to school.
We walk every day after dinner.
Why are you walking so fast?
They walked along the beach at sunset.
We were walking aimlessly through the city.
I will walk with you tomorrow.
Walk straight and turn left.
They would walk more if they had time.

57 – abrir

El banco abre a las nueve.
Abre los ojos.
¿A qué hora abren las tiendas hoy?
Ella abrió su corazón y me contó toda la verdad.
¿Abriste la carta que llegó?
El restaurante abrió hace apenas dos meses.
Abrí los ojos y me di cuenta de que era un sueño.
¿Podrías abrir la puerta? Tengo las manos ocupadas.
No pude abrir la botella de vino sin un sacacorchos.
No pude abrir la lata sin un abrelatas.

to open

The bank opens at nine.
Open your eyes.
What time do the stores open today?
She opened her heart and told me the whole truth.
Did you open the letter that came?
The restaurant opened just two months ago.
I opened my eyes and realized it was a dream.
Could you open the door? My hands are full.
I couldn't open the wine bottle without a corkscrew.
I couldn't open the can without a can opener.

58 – sentarse | **to sit down**

Me siento en la primera fila para ver mejor la obra. | I sit in the front row to see the play better.
¿Dónde nos sentamos? | Where should we sit?
Siéntense, niños, vamos a comer. | Sit down, kids, we're going to eat.
Me senté en el sofá a descansar. | I sat on the couch to rest.
Ella se sentó en la cama a platicar conmigo. | She sat on the bed to chat with me.
Ellos se sentaron en el suelo porque no había sillas. | They sat on the floor because there were no chairs.
Justo nos habíamos sentado cuando empezó a llover. | We had just sat down when it started to rain.
Me sentaré en primera clase si consigo el descuento. | I will sit in first class if I get the discount.
Sentarse bien es importante para la espalda. | Sitting properly is important for your back.
Prefiero sentarme cerca de la ventana. | I prefer to sit near the window.

59 – caer | **to fall**

Me caí de la bicicleta ayer. | I fell off the bicycle yesterday.
Mi cumpleaños cae un sábado este año. | My birthday falls on a Saturday this year.
Caí en la trampa. | I fell into the trap.
El niño se cayó al suelo. | The child fell to the ground.
Se me cayó el vaso y se rompió. | I dropped the glass and it broke.
Están cayendo muchas hojas de los árboles. | Many leaves are falling from the trees.
El perro se cayó del sofá. | The dog fell off the couch.
Esa chica me cae mal. | I don't like that girl.
Me cae bien tu hermano. | I like your brother.
Le caigo bien a sus padres. | His parents like me.

60 – terminar | **to finish, end**

Siempre termino mi tarea antes de cenar. | I always finish my homework before dinner.
¿A qué hora terminas de trabajar? | What time do you finish work?
Mis clases terminan a las tres. | My classes end at three o'clock.
Terminé el libro, y el final me sorprendió. | I finished the book, and the ending surprised me.
¿Ya terminaste tu tarea? | Did you already finish your homework?
La clase terminó temprano. | Class ended early.
Terminamos de comer hace una hora. | We finished eating an hour ago.
No he terminado de leer el libro todavía. | I haven't finished reading the book yet.
Si seguimos así, terminaremos muy tarde. | If we keep going like this, we'll finish really late.
Necesito terminar esto antes de salir. | I need to finish this before going out.

61 – oír	**to hear**
Oigo música en la calle.	I hear music on the street.
¿Oyes eso?	Do you hear that?
Mi abuela no oye bien por el oído izquierdo.	My grandmother doesn't hear well from her left ear.
Se oyen sirenas a lo lejos.	You can hear sirens in the distance.
¿Oíste lo que pasó en el trabajo?	Did you hear what happened at work?
He oído que van a cerrar esa tienda.	I've heard they're going to close that store.
Oímos ruidos raros en el bosque y salimos corriendo.	We heard strange noises in the woods and ran out.
No quiero oír excusas, solo haz lo que te pedí.	I don't want to hear excuses, just do what I asked you.
Me encanta oír la lluvia caer cuando estoy en la cama.	I love hearing the rain fall when I'm in bed.
Quiero oír tu opinión sobre esto.	I want to hear your opinion about this.

62 – cambiar	**to change, exchange**
Cambio de opinión dependiendo de los hechos.	I change my opinion depending on the facts.
El clima cambió de repente.	The weather changed suddenly.
Cambiaron la fecha del evento.	They changed the date of the event.
Cambié de opinión.	I changed my mind.
Todo cambió después del accidente.	Everything changed after the accident.
Cambiamos dólares por euros.	We exchanged dollars for euros.
¿Puedes cambiarme este billete?	Can you exchange this bill for me?
Cámbiate de ropa antes de salir.	Change your clothes before going out.
Cambia tu contraseña regularmente por seguridad.	Change your password regularly for security.
Quiero cambiar mi estilo de vida completamente.	I want to change my lifestyle completely.

63 – limpiar	**to clean**
Limpio el refrigerador una vez al mes.	I clean the refrigerator once a month.
Yo cocino y mi mujer limpia.	I cook and my wife cleans.
Ella siempre limpia su escritorio antes de estudiar.	She always cleans her desk before studying.
Mi abuela siempre está limpiando algo.	My grandma is always cleaning something.
Si tus zapatos están sucios, límpialos antes de entrar.	If your shoes are dirty, clean them before coming in.
¿Ya limpiaste tu cuarto?	Did you clean your room yet?
Ayer limpiamos toda la casa.	Yesterday we cleaned the whole house.
Limpiamos el garaje el fin de semana pasado.	We cleaned the garage last weekend.
Pago a alguien para limpiar mi casa.	I pay someone to clean my house.
Tu tarea es limpiar la mesa después de cenar.	Your chore is to clean the table after eating dinner.

64 – convertir	**to convert, turn into**
El frío convierte el agua en hielo.	The cold turns water into ice.
Este aparato convierte la energía solar en electricidad.	This device converts solar energy into electricity.
El banco convierte pesos en dólares.	The bank converts pesos to dollars.
El agua se convierte en vapor cuando hierve.	Water turns into steam when it boils.
Convertimos el garaje en una oficina.	We converted the garage into an office.
La casa vieja fue convertida en un museo.	The old house was converted into a museum.
Convertí el archivo a PDF.	I converted the file to PDF.
Esa experiencia lo convirtió en un líder.	That experience turned him into a leader.
El escritor convierte sus experiencias en historias.	The writer turns his experiences into stories.
Ella se convirtió al budismo hace cinco años.	She converted to Buddhism five years ago.

65 – mantener	**to maintain, keep**
Siempre mantengo mi teléfono cargado.	I always keep my phone charged.
Mantengo buenas relaciones con mis vecinos.	I maintain good relationships with my neighbors.
Mantengo mi carro en excelente estado.	I keep my car in excellent condition.
Mantén el jardín bien regado en verano.	Keep the garden well-watered in summer.
Él mantiene a su familia trabajando en dos empleos.	He supports his family by working two jobs.
Han mantenido la tradición durante años.	They've maintained the tradition for years.
Es difícil mantener una conversación con tanto ruido.	It's hard to hold a conversation with so much noise.
Hay que mantener la tradición viva.	We must keep the tradition alive.
Trata de mantener el ritmo cuando corras.	Try to maintain the pace when you run.
Es difícil mantener la casa limpia con niños pequeños.	It's hard to keep the house clean with small children.

66 – romper	**to break**
Los niños rompen sus juguetes si juegan muy brusco.	Children break their toys if they play too rough.
Mi hermano rompe las reglas todo el tiempo.	My brother breaks the rules all the time.
¿Por qué rompes todo lo que tocas?	Why do you break everything you touch?
Rompí con mi novia hace dos semanas.	I broke up with my girlfriend two weeks ago.
Rompí un vaso en la cocina.	I broke a glass in the kitchen.
Mi teléfono se rompió cuando se cayó.	My phone broke when it fell.
Los niños rompieron la piñata en cinco minutos.	The kids broke the piñata in five minutes.
He roto dos platos esta semana.	I've broken two plates this week.
Me romperé la espalda si cargo esta caja tan pesada.	I'll break my back if I carry this heavy box.
No quiero romper nada importante.	I don't want to break anything important.

67 – sacar | **to take out, remove, get, take a photo**

Saco la basura todas las noches. | I take out the trash every night.
Mi hija saca muy buenas notas en el colegio. | My daughter gets very good grades at school.
¿Me sacas una foto aquí? | Can you take a picture of me here?
El dentista me sacó una muela ayer. | The dentist pulled out a tooth yesterday.
Se sacaron muchas fotos en la boda. | Many photos were taken at the wedding.
Saqué todo y no encuentro el cargador. | I took everything out and can't find the charger.
¿Sacaste la ropa de la lavadora? | Did you take the clothes out of the washing machine?
Si estudias, sacarás mejor nota en el examen. | If you study, you'll get a better grade on the test.
Te prometo que sacaré mejores notas este semestre. | I promise I'll get better grades this semester.
¿Puedes sacar el pollo del congelador? | Can you take the chicken out of the freezer?

68 – necesitar | **to need**

Necesito hablar contigo un momento. | I need to talk to you for a moment.
No necesito que me digas qué hacer. | I don't need you to tell me what to do.
No necesitas traer nada, tenemos todo. | You don't need to bring anything, we have everything.
Mi hermana necesita dinero para comprar libros. | My sister needs money to buy books.
Necesitamos salir temprano mañana. | We need to leave early tomorrow.
Necesité llamar al médico por el dolor de cabeza. | I needed to call the doctor because of my headache.
Él siempre necesitaba que alguien lo escuchara. | He always needed someone to listen to him.
No he necesitado usar el carro esta semana. | I haven't needed to use the car this week.
¿Necesitaste ayuda para resolver el problema? | Did you need help solving the problem?
¿Crees que va a necesitar cirugía? | Do you think he's going to need surgery?

69 – cocinar | **to cook**

Cocinar es relajante para mí. | Cooking is relaxing for me.
Mi abuela cocina platos tradicionales. | My grandmother cooks traditional dishes.
Aprendí a cocinar con mi abuela. | I learned to cook with my grandmother.
Cuando cocinas para otros, pones amor en la comida. | When you cook for others, you put love into the food.
Ella cocinó una cena deliciosa. | She cooked a delicious dinner.
Estoy cocinando para la familia. | I'm cooking for the family.
No he cocinado nada elaborado últimamente. | I haven't cooked anything elaborate lately.
Cocinamos juntos anoche. | We cooked together last night.
Cocinaré algo especial para tu cumpleaños. | I will cook something special for your birthday.
Cocinaría más a menudo si tuviera más tiempo. | I would cook more often if I had more time.

70 – resultar | **to turn out, prove to be, end up being**

Este trabajo me resulta más difícil de lo que pensaba. | This job is proving to be harder than I thought.
A él siempre le resulta fácil hacer nuevos amigos. | He always finds it easy to make new friends.
Este método resulta útil para bajar de peso. | This method turns out to be useful for losing weight.
Me resultó difícil conseguir trabajo. | It proved to be difficult for me to get a job.
La fiesta resultó un desastre total. | The party turned out to be a total disaster.
La película resultó aburrida, así que nos fuimos antes. | The movie ended up being boring, so we left early.
¿Te ha resultado útil el curso? | Has the course turned out useful for you?
Ha resultado ser una persona muy confiable. | He has turned out to be a very reliable person.
Estoy seguro de que te resultará interesante el tema. | I'm sure you'll find the topic interesting.
No te preocupes, todo va a resultar bien. | Don't worry, everything is going to be fine.

71 – escuchar | **to listen**

Escucho música mientras trabajo. | I listen to music while I work.
¿Me escuchas? | Are you listening to me?
Escúchame. | Listen to me.
Los estudiantes escuchan al profesor. | The students listen to the teacher.
Mi abuela me escucha cuando tengo problemas. | My grandmother listens to me when I have problems.
Ella siempre escucha a sus amigos. | She always listens to her friends.
Tú nunca me escuchas. | You never listen to me.
Aprendí mucho solo escuchando. | I learned a lot just by listening.
Me gusta escuchar podcasts en el carro. | I like listening to podcasts in the car.
¿Te gusta escuchar audiolibros? | Do you like listening to audiobooks?

72 – conseguir | **to obtain, get, achieve**

Él siempre consigue lo que quiere. | He always gets what he wants.
¿Conseguiste las entradas para el concierto? | Did you get the concert tickets?
Conseguí entradas para el concierto. | I got tickets for the concert.
Por fin conseguí lo que quería. | I finally got what I wanted.
Al final ella consiguió el trabajo de sus sueños. | In the end, she got the job of her dreams.
¿Has conseguido el libro que necesitabas? | Have you gotten the book you needed?
Ella consiguió una beca para estudiar en el extranjero. | She got a scholarship to study abroad.
Necesito conseguir un trabajo. | I need to get a job.
Estamos tratando de conseguir una cita. | We're trying to get an appointment.
¿Dónde puedo conseguir un taxi? | Where can I get a taxi?

73 – preparar	**to prepare, get ready**
Mi mamá prepara el desayuno todas las mañanas.	My mom prepares breakfast every morning.
¿Preparas la cena o pido pizza?	Are you making dinner or should I order pizza?
Los estudiantes se preparan para el examen final.	The students are preparing for the final exam.
Estoy preparando la cena.	I'm preparing dinner.
Me estoy preparando para salir.	I'm getting ready to go out.
Preparé la comida y él puso la mesa.	I prepared the meal, and he set the table.
El maestro preparó una actividad divertida.	The teacher prepared a fun activity.
Nos preparamos en cinco minutos.	We got ready in five minutes.
Mañana prepararé algo especial para cenar.	Tomorrow I will prepare something special for dinner.
Tienes que prepararte bien para el examen.	You have to prepare well for the exam.

74 – lograr	**to manage to, achieve, succeed in**
No logro abrir este frasco.	I can't manage to open this jar.
Ella logró entrar a la universidad.	She succeeded in getting into college.
Ella logró sus metas.	She achieved her goals.
¿Lograste dormir bien anoche?	Did you manage to sleep well last night?
Logré terminar el informe antes de la reunión.	I managed to finish the report before the meeting.
Ella logró bajar de peso con dieta y ejercicio.	She managed to lose weight with diet and exercise.
Logramos llegar a tiempo, a pesar del tráfico.	We managed to arrive on time, despite the traffic.
¡Lo logré!	I did it!
Logré convencerlo.	I managed to convince him.
Me cuesta lograr equilibrio entre trabajo y vida.	I find it difficult to achieve a work-life balance.

75 – ocurrir	**to occur, come to mind**
¿Se te ocurre algo?	Does anything come to mind?
No se me ocurre nada para decir en este momento.	Nothing is coming to mind for me to say right now.
Los milagros ocurren cuando menos los esperamos.	Miracles happen when we least expect them.
Nada interesante ocurrió durante la reunión.	Nothing interesting occurred during the meeting.
Se me ocurrió una idea genial.	I had a great idea.
Al salir, se me ocurrió revisar el gas.	On my way out, it occurred to me to check the gas.
El incidente ocurrió la semana pasada.	The incident occurred last week.
La respuesta se le ocurrió justo después del examen.	The answer occurred to him just after the exam.
La ceremonia ocurrirá mañana.	The ceremony will occur tomorrow.
No se me había ocurrido preguntarle a él.	It hadn't occurred to me to ask him.

76 – aparecer	**to appear, show up**
Aparezco brevemente en esa película.	I appear briefly in that movie.
El sol apareció entre las nubes.	The sun appeared through the clouds.
Apareces en todas las fotos de la fiesta.	You show up in all the photos from the party.
Las estrellas aparecen cuando oscurece.	The stars appear when it gets dark.
¿Por qué no apareces nunca cuando te necesito?	Why do you never show up when I need you?
Esa actriz aparece en muchas películas.	That actress appears in many movies.
Aparecieron manchas extrañas en su piel.	Strange spots appeared on her skin.
El mensaje aparece cada vez que inicio sesión.	The message appears every time I log in.
Apareceré en el evento como invitado especial.	I will appear at the event as a special guest.
Tu nombre aparecerá en los créditos finales.	Your name will appear in the final credits.

77 – ganar	**to win, earn**
Gano mucho más dinero que mi marido.	I earn way more money than my husband.
¿Cuánto ganas al mes?	How much do you earn per month?
Ella se gana la vida vendiendo flores en la calle.	She makes a living selling flowers on the street.
Mi hermana siempre gana cuando jugamos ajedrez.	My sister always wins when we play chess.
Ganamos el partido.	We won the game.
Mi equipo ganó el partido anoche.	My team won the game last night.
Ella se ganó el respeto de todos sus colegas.	She earned the respect of all her colleagues.
Él ganó el primer lugar en el concurso.	He won first place in the contest.
Trabajaste duro y te ganaste estas vacaciones.	You worked hard and earned this vacation.
Para ganar experiencia, acepta cualquier trabajo.	To gain experience, accept any job.

78 – acabar	**to finish, end**
Acabé de leer el libro ayer por la noche.	I finished reading the book last night.
La película acaba de una manera inesperada.	The movie ends in an unexpected way.
Cuando acabes tu tarea, puedes salir.	When you finish your homework, you can go out.
Acabo de llegar a casa después del trabajo.	I just got home after work.
La reunión acabó más tarde de lo previsto.	The meeting ended later than expected.
Siempre acabamos discutiendo sobre lo mismo.	We always end up arguing about the same thing.
Acabo de ver a tu hermano.	I just saw your brother.
Si sigues así, acabarás enfermo.	If you continue like this, you'll end up sick.
No sé cómo va a acabar todo esto.	I don't know how all this is going to end.
Se acabó el tiempo.	Time's up.

79 – explicar	**to explain**
Mi profesor explica muy bien matemáticas.	My teacher explains math very well.
Explícame otra vez, no entendí bien.	Explain it to me again, I didn't understand well.
El profesor explicaba con mucha paciencia.	The teacher was explaining very patiently.
Ella me explicó por qué llegó tarde.	She explained to me why she arrived late.
Me explicaron las reglas del juego.	They explained the rules of the game to me.
El doctor nos explicará los resultados mañana.	The doctor will explain the results to us tomorrow.
No sé cómo explicar lo que vi.	I don't know how to explain what I saw.
Es difícil explicar lo que sentí en ese momento.	It's hard to explain what I felt at that moment.
Te voy a explicar el problema paso a paso.	I'm going to explain the problem to you step by step.
¿Puedes explicarme cómo funciona este programa?	Can you explain to me how this program works?

80 – arreglar	**to fix, arrange, settle**
Ella arregla flores para bodas.	She arranges flowers for weddings.
¿Arreglas relojes?	Do you repair watches?
Arreglé la situación con una disculpa.	I settled the situation with an apology.
Mi padre arregló el grifo que goteaba.	My father fixed the leaking faucet.
Los mecánicos arreglaron mi carro ayer.	The mechanics fixed my car yesterday.
Ya arreglé el problema con el WiFi.	I already fixed the WiFi problem.
El plomero arreglará la tubería rota.	The plumber will fix the broken pipe.
Voy a arreglarme el cabello antes de la fiesta.	I'm going to fix my hair before the party.
Yo arreglaría tu computadora si supiera cómo.	I would fix your computer if I knew how.
¿Quieres que te arregle la corbata?	Do you want me to fix your tie?

81 – acercar	**to approach, bring closer**
Acercó la silla a la mesa.	He brought the chair closer to the table.
Me voy a acercar al mostrador para preguntar.	I'm going to approach the counter to ask.
El autobús se acerca a la parada.	The bus is approaching the stop.
El tren ya se está acercando.	The train is already approaching.
El verano se acerca rápidamente.	Summer is approaching quickly.
No te acerques al perro, puede morder.	Don't get close to the dog, it might bite.
Acércate un poco más.	Come a little closer.
Cuando me acerqué, el perro ladró.	When I got closer, the dog barked.
Los niños se acercaron al escenario.	The kids approached the stage.
Nos acercamos al final del año.	We're getting closer to the end of the year.

82 – servir | **to serve, be good for**

Él sirve de ejemplo para los demás. | He serves as an example for others.
Este cuchillo no sirve para cortar pan. | This knife isn't good for cutting bread.
Aquí no sirven desayuno los domingos. | They don't serve breakfast here on Sundays.
¿Para qué sirve esto? | What is this for?
Los voluntarios sirvieron comida a las familias. | The volunteers served food to the families.
Servimos vino tinto con la pasta. | We served red wine with the pasta.
Mi abuela servía las mejores empanadas. | My grandmother served the best empanadas.
No sabía que ya te había servido la comida. | I didn't know you had already been served the food.
¿En qué te puedo servir? | How can I help you?
Quiero servir a mi comunidad. | I want to serve my community.

83 – usar | **to use, wear**

Uso mi celular todo el día. | I use my phone all day.
Ella usa lentes porque no ve bien. | She wears glasses because she can't see well.
¿Qué champú usas para el cabello rizado? | What shampoo do you use for curly hair?
Usamos efectivo porque no aceptan tarjetas aquí. | We use cash because they don't accept cards here.
¿Usaste mi computador sin permiso? | Did you use my computer without permission?
Usé tu baño, espero que no te moleste. | I used your bathroom, I hope you don't mind.
Usamos el GPS, pero igual nos perdimos. | We used the GPS but still got lost.
Antes usaba Facebook, pero ya no. | I used to use Facebook, but not anymore.
He usado tanto esta camisa que ya está gastada. | I've worn this shirt so much it's already worn out.
Prefiero usar transporte público. | I prefer to use public transportation.

84 – tocar | **to touch, knock, play, be one's turn**

¿Tocas algún instrumento? | Do you play an instrument?
Toco el piano todos los días. | I play piano every day.
Me toca lavar los platos hoy. | It's my turn to wash the dishes today.
Te toca pagar la cuenta. | It's your turn to pay the bill.
No toques la pintura, está mojada. | Don't touch the paint, it's wet.
Toqué la puerta y nadie respondió. | I knocked on the door, and no one responded.
Ella tocó el violín en la boda de su hermana. | She played the violin at her sister's wedding.
Cuando yo era niño, tocaba el piano todos los días. | When I was a kid, I used to play the piano every day.
No debiste haber tocado ese botón. | You shouldn't have touched that button.
Nunca he tocado un instrumento. | I've never played an instrument.

85 – ayudar | **to help**

¿Puedes ayudarme con esto? | Can you help me with this?
Estoy aquí para ayudarte. | I'm here to help you.
¿Ayudas a tu hermano con su tarea? | Do you help your brother with his homework?
Ella siempre me ayuda cuando puede. | She always helps me when she can.
Ayudé a mi amigo a mudarse. | I helped my friend move.
Ella ayudó a resolver el problema. | She helped solve the problem.
Te ayudaré mañana. | I will help you tomorrow.
He ayudado mucho en este proyecto. | I have helped a lot in this project.
Agradezco mucho que me hayas ayudado. | I really appreciate that you helped me.
Te ayudaría si pudiera. | I would help you if I could.

86 – mostrar | **to show**

Ella nunca muestra interés en lo que digo. | She never shows interest in what I say.
Los resultados muestran que tenemos razón. | The results show that we're right.
El niño le mostró su dibujo a la profesora. | The child showed his drawing to the teacher.
Le mostré a él las fotos de mis vacaciones. | I showed him the photos from my vacation.
El profesor nos mostró cómo resolver el problema. | The teacher showed us how to solve the problem.
¿Ya le mostraste el dibujo a tu mamá? | Did you already show your mom the drawing?
Te habría mostrado la foto, pero se borró. | I would've shown you the photo, but it got deleted.
Voy a mostrarte algo que te va a encantar. | I'm going to show you something you're going to love.
No quiero mostrar debilidad frente a ellos. | I don't want to show weakness in front of them.
¿Puedes mostrarme cómo se hace esto? | Can you show me how to do this?

87 – estudiar | **to study**

Él estudia todos los días, incluso los fines de semana. | He studies every day, even on weekends.
Estudiamos juntos en la biblioteca todas las tardes. | We study together in the library every afternoon.
Estudian el impacto del cambio climático en la región. | They study the impact of climate change in the region.
Estudié francés cuatro años en el colegio. | I studied French for four years in high school.
Estoy estudiando para el examen de matemáticas. | I'm studying for the math test.
¿Qué estás estudiando en la universidad? | What are you studying at university?
Estudiaron toda la noche para el examen final. | They studied all night for the final exam.
Es importante estudiar con regularidad. | It's important to study regularly.
Él quiere estudiar en el extranjero el próximo año. | He wants to study abroad next year.
Ella quiere estudiar medicina. | She wants to study medicine.

88 – traer | **to bring**
Siempre traigo mi almuerzo desde casa. | I always bring my lunch from home.
¿Me traes un vaso de agua? | Can you bring me a glass of water?
Trae una chaqueta, va a hacer frío. | Bring a jacket, it's going to be cold.
Te traje un recuerdo de nuestro viaje. | I brought you a souvenir from our trip.
¿Quién trajo esta ensalada tan rica? | Who brought this delicious salad?
Trajimos pizza para la reunión. | We brought pizza for the meeting.
He traído todo lo que necesitamos. | I have brought everything we need.
Mi abuela siempre traía dulces cuando venía. | My grandma always brought candy when she came.
¿Traerás a tu novio a la fiesta? | Will you bring your boyfriend to the party?
Voy a traer más café para todos. | I'm going to bring more coffee for everyone.

89 – correr | **to run**
Yo corro todas las mañanas. | I run every morning.
Él corre maratones. | He runs marathons.
Corres muy rápido. | You run very fast.
Mis hijos corren más rápido que yo. | My kids run faster than me.
Corrí cinco kilómetros ayer. | I ran five kilometers yesterday.
Corrí a ayudarla cuando la vi caer. | I ran to help her when I saw her fall.
¿Tú también corriste el maratón? | Did you also run the marathon?
Correré el maratón el próximo mes. | I will run the marathon next month.
Yo correría contigo, pero estoy lesionado. | I would run with you, but I'm injured.
Corríamos juntos en el parque. | We used to run together in the park.

90 – comer | **to eat**
Como frutas y verduras todos los días. | I eat fruits and vegetables every day.
Comes demasiado rápido y eso no es saludable. | You eat too quickly and that's not healthy.
Ella come en ese restaurante cada viernes. | She eats at that restaurant every Friday.
Comemos juntos en familia los domingos. | We eat together as a family on Sundays.
Comimos paella en Valencia. | We ate paella in Valencia.
No he comido nada todavía. | I haven't eaten anything yet.
Comeré algo después del ejercicio. | I will eat something after exercising.
Vamos a comer fuera esta noche. | We're going to eat out tonight.
Me gusta comer saludable. | I like to eat healthy.
Si comieras más sano, te sentirías mejor. | If you ate healthier, you would feel better.

91 – ofrecer | **to offer**

Siempre ofrezco café a mis invitados. | I always offer coffee to my guests.
El hotel ofrece desayuno gratuito todas las mañanas. | The hotel offers free breakfast every morning.
La escuela ofrece clases de inglés por las tardes. | The school offers English classes in the afternoons.
Siempre ofrecemos descuentos en temporada baja. | We always offer discounts in the low season.
Él me ofreció ayuda al verme con las cajas. | He offered me help when he saw me with the boxes.
Me ofrecí para cuidar a los niños mientras ella salía. | I offered to watch the kids while she went out.
Le ofrecieron un trato que no pudo rechazar. | They offered him a deal he couldn't refuse.
¿Te han ofrecido el trabajo ya? | Have they offered you the job yet?
El hotel te ofrecerá una vista increíble del mar. | The hotel will offer you an incredible view of the sea.
Te puedo ofrecer algo de tomar si quieres. | I can offer you something to drink if you want.

92 – levantar | **to get up, lift, raise**

¿A qué hora te levantas? | What time do you get up?
Me levanto a las siete. | I get up at seven.
Levántate ya. | Get up already.
No les levantes la voz a los niños. | Don't raise your voice at the children.
Ella se levantó de la cama lentamente. | She got out of bed slowly.
Levanta la mano si sabes la respuesta. | Raise your hand if you know the answer.
Ella se levantó muy temprano para estudiar. | She got up really early to study.
¿Te cuesta levantarte por la mañana? | Is it hard for you to get up in the morning?
No puedo levantar esta caja, está muy pesada. | I can't lift this box, it's too heavy.
¿Puedes ayudarme a levantar esta caja? | Can you help me lift this box?

93 – jugar | **to play**

Juego al tenis con mi hija cada semana. | I play tennis with my daughter every week.
Mi hijo juega con sus carritos. | My son plays with his toy cars.
Jugamos al fútbol todos los sábados. | We play soccer every Saturday.
Los niños están jugando en el parque. | The kids are playing in the park.
¿Por qué no juegas con tu hermano un rato? | Why don't you play with your brother for a bit?
Los primos estaban jugando a las escondidas. | The cousins were playing hide-and-seek.
Jugaban felices y no querían irse. | They were playing happily and didn't want to leave.
No puedes jugar hasta que termines la tarea. | You can't play until you finish your homework.
¿Sabes jugar ajedrez? | Do you know how to play chess?
No quiero jugar con él, siempre hace trampa. | I don't want to play with him, he always cheats.

94 – comprar | **to buy**

Compro comida dos veces por semana. | I buy food twice per week.
Él compra regalos para todos. | He buys gifts for everyone.
A veces compramos cosas que no necesitamos. | Sometimes we buy things we don't need.
Ellos compraron entradas para el concierto. | They bought tickets for the concert.
¿Dónde compraste esa chaqueta tan bonita? | Where did you buy that pretty jacket?
Yo compraría una casa si tuviera dinero. | I would buy a house if I had money.
Compramos una casa nueva el año pasado. | We bought a new house last year.
Compraré los ingredientes para la cena. | I will buy the ingredients for dinner.
Ella comprará un carro nuevo el mes que viene. | She will buy a new car next month.
Voy a comprarme un libro nuevo. | I'm going to buy myself a new book.

95 – decidir | **to decide**

¿Cómo decides entre tantas opciones? | How do you decide between so many options?
¿Y tú qué decidiste? | And what did you decide?
Decide tú, a mí me da igual. | You decide, it's all the same to me.
Decidí estudiar en el extranjero. | I decided to study abroad.
Al final, decidieron no venir. | In the end, they decided not to come.
¿Has decidido qué vas a hacer? | Have you decided what you're going to do?
Todavía no hemos decidido a dónde ir de vacaciones. | We haven't decided yet where to go on vacation.
Él decidió renunciar a su trabajo. | He decided to quit his job.
Déjame pensarlo antes de decidir. | Let me think about it before deciding.
No puedo decidir entre los dos. | I can't decide between the two.

96 – existir | **to exist**

¿Crees que existe vida en otros planetas? | Do you think life exists on other planets?
¿Existe vida después de la muerte? | Does life exist after death?
Los fantasmas no existen. | Ghosts don't exist.
No existe solución para este problema. | No solution exists for this problem.
No existe una solución perfecta. | There is no perfect solution.
El amor verdadero sí existe. | True love does exist.
No sabía que existía esa posibilidad. | I didn't know that possibility existed.
Los dinosaurios existieron hace millones de años. | Dinosaurs existed millions of years ago.
¿Puede existir amor verdadero sin confianza? | Can true love exist without trust?
Pienso, luego existo. | I think, therefore I am.

97 – alcanzar | **to reach, achieve, attain, catch**

Con mucho esfuerzo, alcancé mi meta. | With a lot of effort, I achieved my goal.
¿Alcanzas el frasco de la estantería? | Can you reach the jar on the shelf?
No pude alcanzarlo antes de que subiera al autobús. | I couldn't catch him before he got on the bus.
Corre más rápido si quieres alcanzarlo. | Run faster if you want to catch up with him.
Alcanzamos la cima de la montaña al amanecer. | We reached the top of the mountain at dawn.
La inflación alcanzó niveles históricos este año. | Inflation reached historic levels this year.
La música alcanzaba la playa. | The music reached the beach.
Alcanzaron un acuerdo tras horas de negociación. | They reached an agreement after hours of negotiation.
El árbol ha alcanzado una altura impresionante. | The tree has reached an impressive height.
Quiero alcanzar un nivel avanzado en español. | I want to reach an advanced level in Spanish.

98 – platicar | **to chat**

Mis papás platican mucho cuando van en el carro. | My parents talk a lot when they're in the car.
Los vecinos platican en la esquina después del trabajo. | The neighbors chat on the corner after work.
¿De qué platican tanto ustedes dos? | What are you two talking about so much?
¿Platicamos cinco minutos antes de entrar? | Can we chat for five minutes before going in?
Mis hijos platican en la cama antes de dormirse. | My kids chat in bed before falling asleep.
Platicamos un buen rato después de cenar. | We chatted for a while after dinner.
Mientras cocinábamos, platicábamos de todo. | While we cooked, we talked about everything.
Platicaban en la cocina tomando café. | They were chatting in the kitchen drinking coffee.
Oye, platícame qué pasó. | Hey, tell me what happened.
Mi tía me llama para platicar chismes del pueblo. | My aunt calls me to chat about town gossip.

99 – pagar | **to pay**

Pago el alquiler el primer día del mes. | I pay the rent on the first day of the month.
La empresa paga muy bien a sus empleados. | The company pays its employees very well.
Mis padres pagan la universidad. | My parents pay for college.
Pagué demasiado por este carro. | I paid too much for this car.
¿Cuánto pagaste por esa camisa? | How much did you pay for that shirt?
Pagaban muy mal en ese trabajo, por eso renuncié. | They paid really poorly at that job, so I quit.
¿Te pagaron por las horas extras? | Did they pay you for the overtime?
Pagaré la multa mañana. | I'll pay the fine tomorrow.
¿Puedo pagar con mi teléfono? | Can I pay with my phone?
¿Vas a pagar en efectivo o con tarjeta? | Are you going to pay cash or with a card?

100 – meter	**to put in**
Mete la ropa en la lavadora.	Put the clothes in the washing machine.
Mete la comida en el refrigerador.	Put the food in the refrigerator.
No te metas en eso.	Don't get involved in that.
Metí la carta en el buzón esta mañana.	I put the letter in the mailbox this morning.
Me metí en un lío.	I got myself into trouble.
El niño se metió el juguete en la boca.	The child put the toy in his mouth.
Metieron al ladrón en la cárcel.	They put the thief in jail.
No quiero meterme en problemas.	I don't want to get into trouble.
Me voy a meter en la ducha.	I'm going to get in the shower.
¿Puedes meter eso en el cajón?	Can you put that in the drawer?

101 – cumplir	**to have a birthday, turn an age**
Mañana cumplo treinta años.	Tomorrow I turn 30 years old.
Mi hijo cumple cinco años el próximo mes.	My son turns five years old next month.
Vamos a celebrar porque Juan cumple dieciocho años.	We're going to celebrate because Juan is turning 18.
Cumplí cuarenta la semana pasada.	I turned 40 last week.
Mi abuela cumple noventa y haremos una fiesta.	My grandmother is turning 90 and we'll have a party.
Mi hija cumplió cinco años ayer.	My daughter turned five yesterday.
Mi hijo cumple siete años hoy.	My son turns seven today.
Voy a cumplir años la próxima semana.	I'm going to have my birthday next week.
¿Cuántos años vas a cumplir?	How old are you going to be?
Cumpliré cuarenta y cinco años la próxima semana.	I will turn forty-five years old next week.

102 – encantar	**to love**
Me encanta el chocolate.	I love chocolate.
A ella le encanta jugar al fútbol.	She loves to play soccer.
Nos encanta viajar juntos.	We love traveling together.
Les encanta esa película.	They love that movie.
Me encantó tu regalo.	I loved your gift.
De niño, me encantaba jugar en el parque.	As a child, I used to love playing in the park.
Me encantaría visitar Japón algún día.	I would love to visit Japan someday.
Nos encantaría conocerte.	We'd love to meet you.
Te encantará este restaurante.	You will love this restaurant.
Nos encantaría poder viajar más seguido.	We'd love to be able to travel more often.

103 – continuar | **to continue**

El conflicto continúa sin resolver. | The conflict continues unresolved.
Él continuó trabajando a pesar de su enfermedad. | He continued working despite his illness.
Él continuó su camino sin mirar atrás. | He continued on his way without looking back.
Continuaremos con la reunión después del almuerzo. | We'll continue with the meeting after lunch.
Después del descanso, continuaremos con la reunión. | After the break, we will continue with the meeting.
¿Desea continuar con la instalación? | Do you want to continue with the installation?
El programa continuará hasta fin de año. | The program will continue until the end of the year.
El juicio continuará el lunes. | The trial will continue on Monday.
Quiero continuar mis estudios en el extranjero. | I want to continue my studies abroad.
Por favor, continúe por este camino. | Please continue along this path.

104 – pelear | **to fight**

Ella siempre pelea con su hermana por cosas tontas. | She always fights with her sister over silly things.
Mis hijos siempre se pelean por el control remoto. | My kids always fight over the remote control.
Si siguen peleando, los voy a separar. | If you keep fighting, I'm going to separate you.
Me peleé con mi mejor amigo. | I had a fight with my best friend.
Él peleó por horas con su novia anoche. | He fought for hours with his girlfriend last night.
¿Te has peleado con un compañero de trabajo? | Have you fought with a coworker?
Los niños se pelearon en el recreo. | The kids got into a fight during recess.
Pelearemos por conseguir mejores salarios. | We will fight to get better salaries.
No vale la pena pelear por eso. | It's not worth fighting over that.
No quiero pelear contigo por algo tan tonto. | I don't want to fight with you over something so silly.

105 – dormir | **to sleep**

Yo siempre duermo ocho horas. | I always sleep eight hours.
Él duerme como un bebé. | He sleeps like a baby.
Mis padres duermen en habitaciones separadas. | My parents sleep in separate rooms.
De niño, dormía con un peluche. | As a child, I slept with a stuffed animal.
Anoche dormí muy mal. | Last night I slept very badly.
Ella durmió diez horas seguidas. | She slept for ten hours straight.
¿Dormiste bien anoche? | Did you sleep well last night?
Los niños dormirán en casa de su abuela. | The kids will sleep at their grandma's house.
Los niños están durmiendo. | The children are sleeping.
Nos gusta dormir hasta tarde los domingos. | We like to sleep in on Sundays.

106 – agarrar | **to grab, catch, hold**

Necesito agarrar mis llaves antes de salir. | I need to grab my keys before leaving.
Agarra el paraguas, está lloviendo. | Grab the umbrella, it's raining.
La policía logró agarrar al ladrón. | The police managed to catch the thief.
Lo agarraron robando. | They caught him stealing.
Agarramos el último tren. | We caught the last train.
Agarra mi mano para cruzar la calle. | Hold my hand to cross the street.
Él se agarró de la baranda para no caer. | He held onto the railing to avoid falling.
Ella agarró el vaso antes de que se cayera. | She grabbed the glass before it fell.
Agarra bien el volante cuando conduzcas. | Hold the steering wheel firmly when you drive.
¿Puedes agarrar eso por mí? | Can you grab that for me?

107 – subir | **to go up, raise, climb, get in, upload**

Siempre subo corriendo las escaleras. | I always run up the stairs.
Mi hermana sube fotos a Instagram todos los días. | My sister uploads photos to Instagram every day.
Los precios de la gasolina suben cada semana. | Gas prices go up every week.
Súbete al carro que ya nos vamos. | Get in the car, we're leaving now.
Subí hasta la cima de la montaña. | I climbed to the top of the mountain.
Mi papá me subió a sus hombros para que pudiera ver. | My dad raised me onto his shoulders so I could see.
Ya subieron los precios otra vez. | They raised the prices again.
Me subía a los árboles cuando era niño. | I used to climb trees when I was a kid.
Los impuestos subirán el próximo año. | Taxes will go up next year.
Mi abuela no puede subir sola al segundo piso. | My grandmother can't go up to the second floor alone.

108 – intentar | **to try, attempt**

Él siempre intenta hacer las cosas bien. | He always tries to do things right.
Intenté seguir las instrucciones. | I tried to follow the instructions.
¿Por qué no lo intentas? | Why don't you try it?
¿Intentaste solicitar la beca? | Did you try applying for the scholarship?
Intenté llamarte tres veces ayer. | I tried to call you three times yesterday.
Intenté abrir la puerta, pero estaba cerrada con llave. | I tried to open the door, but it was locked.
Lo intenté varias veces. | I tried it several times.
El paciente intentó suicidarse. | The patient attempted suicide.
El ladrón intentó escapar por la ventana. | The thief tried to escape through the window.
Voy a intentar terminar el trabajo hoy. | I'm going to try to finish the work today.

109 – descubrir — **to find out, discover**

Descubres cosas de ti mismo con el tiempo. — You discover things about yourself over time.
¿Cristóbal Colón descubrió América? — Did Christopher Columbus discover America?
¿Has descubierto algo nuevo? — Have you discovered anything new?
Descubrí que él me había mentido. — I discovered that he lied to me.
Todavía no he descubierto cómo funciona. — I still haven't discovered how it works.
Descubrirás que no es tan difícil. — You will discover that it's not so difficult.
Los científicos descubrieron una nueva especie. — Scientists discovered a new species.
Descubrimos una playa escondida. — We discovered a hidden beach.
Quiero descubrir qué pasó. — I want to find out what happened.
Acabo de descubrir un restaurante increíble. — I just discovered an amazing restaurant.

110 – olvidar — **to forget**

Siempre olvido dónde pongo las llaves del carro. — I always forget where I put the car keys.
No olvides llamar a tu mamá. — Don't forget to call your mom.
Mi abuela está olvidando muchas cosas últimamente. — My grandmother is forgetting many things lately.
Olvidé mi celular. — I forgot my cell phone.
Se me olvidó comprar leche en el supermercado. — I forgot to buy milk at the supermarket.
Olvidamos el cumpleaños de Ana. — We forgot Ana's birthday.
¿Te has olvidado de llamar a tu mamá? — Have you forgotten to call your mom?
Nunca olvidaré a mi primer amor. — I'll never forget my first love.
Quiero olvidar esa experiencia. — I want to forget that experience.
Olvídalo, ya no importa lo que pasó. — Forget it, what happened doesn't matter anymore.

111 – incluir — **to include**

Me incluyo en las personas que prefieren café. — I include myself among people who prefer coffee.
No incluyas información personal en el correo. — Don't include personal information in the email.
El paquete incluye transporte al aeropuerto. — The package includes transportation to the airport.
El informe incluye los datos más recientes. — The report includes the most recent data.
Incluimos ejercicios de calentamiento en la rutina. — We include warm-up exercises in the routine.
¿Está incluido el desayuno en el precio? — Is breakfast included in the price?
El precio incluye el desayuno. — The price includes breakfast.
Él se incluyó en el equipo sin preguntar. — He included himself on the team without asking.
¿Puedes incluirme en el grupo? — Can you include me in the group?
Debemos incluir más verduras en nuestra dieta. — We should include more vegetables in our diet.

112 – andar | **to walk around, wander, go**

El turista anduvo por el centro histórico. | The tourist wandered around the historic center.
Anduvimos por el centro toda la tarde. | We wandered around downtown all afternoon.
Anduve por el centro comercial sin rumbo fijo. | I wandered around the mall with no fixed direction.
Anduvimos todo el día buscando un buen restaurante. | We wandered all day looking for a good restaurant.
¿Cómo ha andado tu mamá de salud? | How's your mother's health been?
El negocio ha estado andando de mal en peor este año. | Business has been going from bad to worse this year.
Tu hijo está andando con malas compañías. | Your son is going around with the wrong crowd.
Él anda contento desde que consiguió el ascenso. | He's been happy ever since he got promoted.
Últimamente he andado muy cansado. | Lately I've been very tired.
¿Dónde andabas ayer? No te vi. | Where were you yesterday? I didn't see you.

113 – nacer | **to be born**

Si naces en una familia grande, aprendes a compartir. | If you're born into a large family, you learn to share.
Los bebés nacen cuando están listos. | Babies are born when they're ready.
Los líderes nacen, no se hacen. | Leaders are born, not made.
¿Dónde naciste? | Where were you born?
Nací en abril durante una gran tormenta. | I was born in April during a big storm.
Mi abuelo nació en un pueblo pequeño de México. | My grandfather was born in a small town in Mexico.
Él nació en Colombia, pero creció en España. | He was born in Colombia but grew up in Spain.
Mi primer hijo nació por cesárea. | My first child was born by cesarean section.
Los gemelos nacieron con dos minutos de diferencia. | The twins were born two minutes apart.
Los pollitos acaban de nacer esta mañana. | The chicks were just born this morning.

114 – aprender | **to learn**

¿Dónde aprendiste a hablar español? | Where did you learn to speak Spanish?
¿Quién te enseñó? ¿O lo aprendiste tú solo? | Who taught you? Or did you learn it yourself?
Aprendo español por mi cuenta. | I learn Spanish on my own.
Aprender un idioma requiere tiempo y paciencia. | Learning a language takes time and patience.
Los niños aprenden rápido. | Kids learn quickly.
Me gusta aprender cosas nuevas cada día. | I like to learn new things every day.
Aprendí a cocinar viendo videos. | I learned to cook by watching videos.
Aprendí a nadar cuando tenía cinco años. | I learned to swim when I was five years old.
Aprendiste muchas cosas útiles en ese curso. | You learned many useful things in that course.
Aprendieron a hablar español en solo seis meses. | They learned to speak Spanish in just six months.

115 – dedicar

Dedico dos horas diarias al ejercicio.
¿A qué te dedicas?
Me dedico a la enseñanza.
Ella dedica su vida a ayudar a los demás.
Dediqué la tarde a estudiar para el examen.
El autor dedicó su libro a sus hijos.
Dedicaron la obra a su profesor.
Voy a dedicar el fin de semana a descansar.
No tengo tiempo para dedicarme a eso ahora.
Quiero dedicar esta canción a mi madre.

to dedicate

I dedicate two hours daily to exercise.
What do you do for a living?
I work in education.
She dedicates her life to helping others.
I dedicated the afternoon to studying for the exam.
The author dedicated his book to his children.
They dedicated the work to their teacher.
I'm going to devote the weekend to resting.
I don't have time to devote myself to that now.
I want to dedicate this song to my mother.

116 – suponer

Supongo que tienes razón.
Supongo que sí.
¿Qué supones que va a pasar?
Supuse que no estabas interesado.
Él nunca supuso que le mentían.
Supusimos que el examen sería más fácil.
Supondría que está ocupado si no responde.
Ya había supuesto que ibas a decir eso.
Supón que todo sale mal, ¿qué harías?
Nunca debimos suponer que iba a funcionar.

to suppose, assume, guess, imply

I suppose you're right.
I suppose so.
What do you think is going to happen?
I assumed you weren't interested.
He never assumed they were lying to him.
We assumed the exam would be easier.
I'd assume he's busy if he doesn't answer.
I had already assumed you were going to say that.
Let's say everything goes wrong, what would you do?
We never should have assumed it was going to work.

117 – aceptar

Tengo que aceptar que cometí un error.
Debes aceptar las consecuencias de tus acciones.
No puedo aceptar ese regalo, es demasiado.
Ella aceptó el trabajo sin dudarlo.
La empresa no puede aceptar más pedidos este mes.
Por favor, acepta mis sinceras disculpas.
¿Aceptas efectivo o solo tarjeta?
Acepté que no todo sale como uno espera.
Ella fue aceptada en la universidad.
No todos aceptan las críticas de buena manera.

to accept

I have to accept that I made a mistake.
You must accept the consequences of your actions.
I can't accept that gift, it's too much.
She accepted the job without hesitation.
The company cannot accept more orders this month.
Please accept my sincere apologies.
Do you accept cash or only card?
I accepted that not everything turns out as you expect.
She was accepted into the university.
Not everyone accepts criticism in a good way.

118 – comprender	**to understand**
No comprendo lo que estás diciendo.	I don't understand what you're saying.
Comprendes el español bastante bien.	You understand Spanish quite well.
Comprendemos tus preocupaciones.	We understand your concerns.
A veces los niños no comprenden las reglas.	Sometimes kids don't understand the rules.
Al principio no lo comprendí, pero ahora sí.	At first I didn't understand it, but now I do.
¿Comprendiste lo que explicó el profesor?	Did you understand what the teacher explained?
Ellos comprendieron la explicación inmediatamente.	They understood the explanation immediately.
Comprenderás mejor cuando seas mayor.	You will understand better when you're older.
Comprendería tu decisión si me explicaras por qué.	I'd understand your decision if you explained why.
Estoy tratando de comprender tus sentimientos.	I'm trying to understand your feelings.

119 – obtener	**to get, obtain**
Obtengo un certificado al finalizar el curso.	I get a certificate at the end of the course.
Mi hermano obtuvo su licencia de conducir.	My brother got his driver's license.
Él obtuvo su pasaporte en solo dos semanas.	He got his passport in just two weeks.
¿Qué resultados obtuviste del experimento?	What results did you get from the experiment?
Los estudiantes obtuvieron buenas calificaciones.	The students got good grades.
Obtuvimos permiso del director.	We got the principal's permission.
Obtendré mi título universitario en mayo.	I will get my college degree in May.
Para obtener la beca, llena esta solicitud.	To get the scholarship, fill out this application.
¿Dónde puedo obtener información sobre el curso?	Where can I get information about the course?
Puedes obtener más información en el sitio web.	You can get more information on the website.

120 – cuidar	**to take care of, look after**
Cuido mi salud haciendo ejercicio regularmente.	I take care of my health by exercising regularly.
Yo cuido a mis padres ancianos.	I take care of my elderly parents.
Mi madre cuida a los niños mientras trabajamos.	My mother takes care of the children while we work.
Yo cuidé a mi hermano cuando estuvo enfermo.	I took care of my brother when he was sick.
Mis abuelos me cuidaron cuando era pequeño.	My grandparents looked after me when I was little.
Cuidaron la casa mientras estábamos de viaje.	They looked after the house while we were traveling.
Cuídate mucho.	Take good care of yourself.
Cuidaré de todo mientras no estés.	I will take care of everything while you're away.
Cuidar a alguien requiere paciencia.	Taking care of someone requires patience.
¿Puedes cuidar mis plantas mientras estoy de viaje?	Can you look after my plants while I'm traveling?

121 – formar	to form, train oneself
La familia forma el núcleo de la sociedad.	The family forms the core of society.
Los estudiantes forman grupos de cuatro personas.	The students form groups of four people.
Los alumnos formaron una fila frente al salón.	The students formed a line in front of the classroom.
Quieren formar una banda de música.	They want to form a music band.
Vamos a formar un equipo para el proyecto.	We're going to form a team for the project.
Me formé como abogado en la Universidad Nacional.	I trained as a lawyer at the National University.
El carácter se forma desde la infancia.	Character is shaped from childhood.
Ella se formó en administración de empresas.	She trained in business administration.
Me estoy formando como programador.	I'm training as a programmer.
Los médicos se forman durante años.	Doctors train for years.

122 – echar	to pour, throw (often used idiomatically)
Echa un poco más de aceite en la ensalada.	Pour a little more oil on the salad.
¿Le has echado gasolina al carro?	Have you put gas in the car?
Siempre me echa la culpa a mí.	He always blames me.
Mis padres me echaron de casa.	My parents kicked me out of the house.
¿Me puedes echar una mano con esto?	Can you give me a hand with this?
¿Puedes echarle un ojo al horno?	Can you keep an eye on the oven?
Me voy a echar una siesta rápida.	I'm going to take a quick nap.
Echa un vistazo a este documento.	Take a look at this document.
Echar piedras no es buena idea.	Throwing stones is not a good idea.
Echar a andar el carro fue fácil.	Getting the car going was easy.

123 – responder	to respond, answer, reply
Siempre le respondo a mi mamá cuando me llama.	I always answer my mom when she calls me.
¿Por qué no respondes mis mensajes?	Why don't you reply to my messages?
Él no está respondiendo al tratamiento.	He's not responding to treatment.
Responde con sinceridad.	Answer honestly.
Te respondí apenas vi el mensaje.	I answered you as soon as I saw the message.
¿Ya le respondiste al jefe?	Did you already reply to the boss?
Ella me respondió de mala manera.	She answered me rudely.
Ellos me respondieron muy rápido por correo.	They replied to me very quickly by email.
¿Crees que nos responderán antes del viernes?	Do you think they'll respond to us before Friday?
No sé cómo responder a esa pregunta.	I don't know how to respond to that question.

124 – mover | **to move**

Mueve la mesa hacia la ventana, por favor. | Move the table toward the window, please.
Mi abuela ya no se mueve como antes. | My grandmother doesn't move around like before.
Cuando ella baila, se mueve con mucha gracia. | When she dances, she moves with a lot of grace.
No te muevas, que te estoy tomando una foto. | Don't move, I'm taking a picture of you.
Los niños se mueven mucho durante la clase. | The children move around a lot during class.
Me moví rápido para no llegar tarde. | I moved quickly so I wouldn't be late.
¿Quién movió mis cosas? No estaban así. | Who moved my things? They weren't like this.
Movimos todos los muebles para limpiar la casa. | We moved all the furniture to clean the house.
No puedo mover el brazo, me duele mucho. | I can't move my arm, it hurts a lot.
Voy a mover el carro para que puedas salir. | I'm going to move the car so you can get out.

125 – presentar | **to present, introduce, show up**

La empresa presenta los resultados mañana. | The company presents results tomorrow.
El paciente presenta síntomas de gripe. | The patient is showing flu symptoms.
Me presenté al examen sin estudiar mucho. | I showed up to the exam without studying much.
Mi amigo me presentó a su novia en la fiesta. | My friend introduced me to his girlfriend at the party.
El abogado presentó pruebas nuevas durante el juicio. | The lawyer presented new evidence during the trial.
Nos presentaron en una reunión de trabajo. | They introduced us at a work meeting.
De niño, me presentaba como Superman. | As a kid, I introduced myself as Superman.
El alcalde presentará el plan la próxima semana. | The mayor will present the plan next week.
Presenta tu identificación en la entrada. | Present your identification at the entrance.
Quiero presentarte a mis padres. | I want to introduce you to my parents.

126 – señalar | **to point out**

Mi mamá siempre señala mis errores. | My mom always points out my mistakes.
Los estudios señalan que el ejercicio es importante. | Studies indicate that exercise is important.
¿Por qué me señalas si yo no fui? | Why are you pointing at me if it wasn't me?
Como señalaste ayer, necesitamos más tiempo. | As you pointed out yesterday, we need more time.
Señalé mi casa a los nuevos vecinos. | I pointed out my house to the new neighbors.
El profesor señaló mi error con mucha paciencia. | The teacher pointed out my mistake very patiently.
Ella señaló que no estaba de acuerdo. | She pointed out that she didn't agree.
Ya he señalado que eso no funciona. | I've already pointed out that it doesn't work.
Le hemos señalado los errores en el contrato. | We've pointed out the errors in the contract to him.
¿Puedes señalar en el mapa dónde estamos? | Can you point on the map where we are?

127 – suceder | **to happen, occur**

¿Qué sucede si no tomo la medicina? What happens if I don't take the medicine?
Eso sucede cuando no duermes bien. That happens when you don't sleep well.
Las cosas suceden por una razón. Things happen for a reason.
Sucedió un terremoto en Chile. An earthquake happened in Chile.
Le sucedieron cosas terribles durante la guerra. Terrible things happened to him during the war.
Todo sucedió tan rápido que no me di cuenta. Everything happened so fast that I didn't realize.
Nunca me ha sucedido nada tan increíble. Nothing so incredible has ever happened to me.
Sucedían muchas cosas raras en esa casa. A lot of strange things used to happen in that house.
Estoy seguro de que sucederá algo bueno. I'm sure something good will happen.
Nadie esperaba que algo así pudiera suceder. No one expected something like that could happen.

128 – bajar | **to go down, lower, download**

¿Puedes bajar el volumen? Can you turn the volume down?
¿Cómo se baja este programa? How do you download this program?
Bajamos del tren en la próxima estación. We get off the train at the next station.
Bajé los archivos del sitio web. I downloaded the files from the website.
Mi padre bajó del avión hace una hora. My father got off the plane an hour ago.
Bajamos al primer piso. We went down to the first floor.
El gato no puede bajar del árbol. The cat can't get down from the tree.
¿Puedes ayudarme a bajar esta aplicación? Can you help me download this app?
Bajaré a comprar pan por la mañana. I will go down to buy bread in the morning.
Baja la cabeza cuando pases por esa puerta. Lower your head when you go through that door.

129 – evitar | **to avoid**

Evito esa calle porque hay mucho tráfico. I avoid that street because there's too much traffic.
Ella evita hablar de política con la familia. She avoids talking about politics with family.
Evitamos el tráfico saliendo más temprano de casa. We avoid traffic by leaving home earlier.
Evité hablar con él para prevenir una discusión. I avoided talking to him to prevent an argument.
Evitaron mencionar el tema durante la cena. They avoided mentioning the topic during dinner.
Yo evitaría esa película si no te gusta el terror. I would avoid that movie if you don't like horror.
Ella evitó responder a la pregunta. She avoided answering the question.
Evitaremos viajar en Navidad. We will avoid traveling at Christmas.
La vacuna ayuda a evitar enfermedades graves. The vaccine helps to avoid serious illnesses.
Evita comer antes de nadar. Avoid eating before swimming.

130 – asegurar | **to ensure, insure, secure, assure**

Quiero asegurar una buena educación para mis hijos. | I want to ensure a good education for my children.
Te aseguro que todo saldrá bien. | I assure you everything will turn out fine.
Te aseguro que estará listo mañana. | I assure you it'll be ready tomorrow.
Aseguran que el evento será un éxito. | They assure that the event will be a success.
La póliza asegura tu carro contra robos. | The policy insures your car against theft.
Aseguramos la casa antes del huracán. | We secured the house before the hurricane.
Aseguré las ventanas antes de la tormenta. | I secured the windows before the storm.
El gobierno aseguraba que todo mejoraría. | The government assured everything would improve.
Ellos se aseguraron de cerrar bien la oficina. | They made sure to close the office properly.
Asegúrate de apagar las luces. | Make sure you turn off the lights.

131 – imaginar | **to imagine**

No me imagino la vida sin mi celular. | I can't imagine life without my cell phone.
Los niños imaginan mundos fantásticos jugando. | Children imagine fantastic worlds while playing.
Imagínate que te ganas la lotería. | Imagine if you won the lottery.
Me imaginé que te gustaría. | I imagined that you would like it.
Siempre imaginé que sería doctora. | I always imagined I'd be a doctor.
No imaginé que sería tan difícil. | I didn't imagine it would be this hard.
No me imaginaba que el restaurante fuera tan caro. | I didn't imagine the restaurant would be so expensive.
Me gusta imaginar finales alternativos a las películas. | I like imagining alternate endings to movies.
Me cuesta imaginar la vida sin internet. | It's hard for me to imagine life without the internet.
No puedo imaginar la vida sin música. | I can't imagine life without music.

132 – detener | **to detain, halt, stop**

El juez detuvo el procedimiento. | The judge halted the proceedings.
La policía detuvo al sospechoso. | The police detained the suspect.
La construcción se detuvo indefinidamente. | Construction was halted indefinitely.
Detuvieron al ladrón después del robo. | They arrested the thief after the robbery.
El guardia detuvo el carro en la entrada. | The guard stopped the car at the entrance.
El tren se detuvo de repente. | The train stopped suddenly.
Están deteniendo a todos los vehículos. | They are stopping all vehicles.
Los manifestantes detuvieron el tráfico. | The protesters stopped the traffic.
Frenó el carro, pero no logró detenerlo a tiempo. | He braked the car but didn't manage to stop it in time.
El presidente pidió detener el proyecto. | The president asked to halt the project.

133 – sufrir | **to suffer**

Sufro de dolor de espalda. | I suffer from back pain.
Mi papá sufre de diabetes. | My dad suffers from diabetes.
Muchos jóvenes sufren baja autoestima. | Many young people suffer from low self-esteem.
Él está sufriendo por la muerte de su madre. | He's suffering over his mother's death.
Sufrí mucho durante esa relación tóxica. | I suffered a lot during that toxic relationship.
El equipo sufrió una derrota humillante. | The team suffered a humiliating defeat.
Cuando yo era niño, sufría de asma. | When I was a child, I suffered from asthma.
Mi mamá ha sufrido de migrañas desde hace años. | My mom has suffered from migraines for years.
Si no te cuidas, sufrirás después. | If you don't take care of yourself, you'll suffer later.
Es normal sufrir nervios antes de una entrevista. | It's normal to feel nervous before an interview.

134 – importar | **to matter, import**

No me importa. | I don't care.
¿Te importa si cierro la ventana? | Do you mind if I close the window?
Lo que más me importa es que estés bien. | What matters most to me is that you're okay.
¿Te importa lo que pasó ayer? | Do you care about what happened yesterday?
No importa si llegas tarde, yo te espero. | It doesn't matter if you're late; I'll wait for you.
Estados Unidos importa aguacates de México. | The United States imports avocados from Mexico.
El país importa más de lo que exporta. | The country imports more than it exports.
No importa si llueve, iremos igual. | It doesn't matter if it rains, we'll go anyway.
No importa el precio, lo quiero. | The price doesn't matter, I want it.
Lo que importa es que estés bien. | What matters is that you're okay.

135 – ocupar | **to take up, occupy, take care of, handle**

Yo me ocupo de traer las bebidas. | I'll handle bringing the drinks.
¿Te ocupas de cerrar la casa? | Will you take care of locking up the house?
Ella se ocupa de todo lo relacionado con el evento. | She handles everything related to the event.
La mesa ocupa demasiado lugar en la cocina. | The table takes up too much space in the kitchen.
Me ocupé de enviar todos los correos esta mañana. | I took care of sending all the emails this morning.
El ejército ocupó la zona después del conflicto. | The army occupied the area after the conflict.
Los estudiantes ocuparon el edificio en protesta. | The students occupied the building in protest.
Me estoy ocupando de los últimos detalles de la boda. | I'm handling the final details of the wedding.
No te preocupes, yo me ocuparé de eso mañana. | Don't worry, I'll take care of that tomorrow.
Esta reunión va a ocupar toda la tarde. | This meeting is going to take up the whole afternoon.

136 – manejar — **to drive, handle**

¿Manejas tu o manejo yo?	Are you driving or am I?
¿Cómo manejas tanto estrés?	How do you handle so much stress?
Ella maneja muy bien el estrés.	She handles stress very well.
Aprendí a manejar cuando tenía dieciséis años.	I learned to drive when I was 16.
Manejé hasta tu casa pero no estabas.	I drove to your house, but you weren't there.
Manejamos cuatro horas seguidas.	We drove for four hours straight.
Nunca he manejado un camión tan grande.	I've never driven such a big truck.
¿Puedes manejar tú? Estoy cansado.	Can you drive? I'm tired.
No me gusta manejar de noche.	I don't like driving at night.
Me encanta manejar de noche porque hay poco tráfico.	I love driving at night because there's little traffic.

137 – bañar — **to bathe**

Tengo que bañar al bebé.	I have to bathe the baby.
Me baño todas las noches.	I take a bath every night.
La madre baña a su bebé con cuidado.	The mother bathes her baby carefully.
El sol baña la habitación con su luz.	The sun bathes the room with its light.
Él está bañando al gato y está enojado.	He's bathing the cat and it's angry.
Ellos se bañan en la playa todos los días.	They swim at the beach every day.
Bañé al perro después del paseo.	I bathed the dog after the walk.
Me baño todos los días, sin falta.	I shower every day, without fail.
Se bañaban juntos cuando eran niños.	They used to bathe together as kids.
Nos bañaremos en las aguas termales.	We will bathe in the thermal waters.

138 – repetir — **to repeat, do again, have seconds**

Siempre repito los mismos errores.	I always repeat the same mistakes.
La historia se repite.	History repeats itself.
No repitas lo que te dije.	Don't repeat what I told you.
Repetí la pregunta, pero él no respondió.	I repeated the question, but he didn't answer.
El profesor repitió la explicación.	The teacher repeated the explanation.
Mi abuela repetía esa historia en cada visita.	My grandmother would repeat that story every visit.
He repetido este ejercicio, pero no me sale.	I've repeated this exercise, but I can't get it right.
No repetiré ese error nunca más.	I will never repeat that mistake again.
¿Vas a repetir postre?	Are you going for seconds on dessert?
¿Puedes repetir lo que dijiste?	Can you repeat what you said?

139 – cerrar — **to close**

La tienda cierra a las ocho. — The store closes at eight.
Ella cierra los ojos al meditar. — She closes her eyes when meditating.
Los parques cierran al atardecer. — Parks close at sunset.
Cerramos temprano los domingos. — We close early on Sundays.
El banco ya ha cerrado por hoy. — The bank has already closed for the day.
El banco cerrará mañana por ser feriado. — The bank will be closed tomorrow due to the holiday.
Cerraré la cuenta si hay problemas. — I will close the account if there are problems.
La biblioteca cerrará temprano hoy. — The library will close early today.
Asegúrate de cerrarlo bien. — Make sure to shut it properly.
Habían cerrado el trato antes de que yo llegara. — They had closed the deal before my arrival.

140 – faltar — **to be missing, be lacking**

Nos falta información para tomar una decisión. — We lack the information to make a decision.
¿Te falta algo? — Are you missing anything?
Me falta dinero para comprar el carro. — I need money to buy the car.
A esta sopa le falta sal. — This soup needs salt.
Me faltan cinco pesos. — I'm short five pesos.
Él nunca falta a los entrenamientos. — He never misses practice.
¿Quién falta en la lista? — Who's missing from the list?
Faltan tres días para el examen. — There are three days left until the exam.
Falta poco para las vacaciones. — Vacation time is almost here.
¿Cuánto falta para llegar? — How much longer until we get there?

141 – indicar — **to indicate**

La brújula indica el norte magnético. — The compass indicates magnetic north.
El formulario indica dónde debes firmar. — The form indicates where you should sign.
Los análisis indican niveles altos de colesterol. — The tests indicate high cholesterol levels.
Todo indica que va a llover. — Everything indicates it's going to rain.
El mapa indica dónde están los baños. — The map points out where the bathrooms are.
El letrero indica que no se debe fumar aquí. — The sign indicates that you shouldn't smoke here.
Su comportamiento indica nerviosismo. — His behavior indicates nervousness.
Los datos indican una tendencia positiva. — The data indicates a positive trend.
¿Qué síntomas indican una infección? — What symptoms indicate an infection?
El guía nos indicó el camino correcto. — The guide pointed us to the right path.

142 – vender	**to sell**
Vendo empanadas caseras.	I sell homemade empanadas.
Esta tienda vende de todo.	This store sells everything.
Los domingos vendemos tamales en el parque.	On Sundays we sell tamales in the park.
Vendí mi bicicleta porque ya no la usaba.	I sold my bike because I wasn't using it anymore.
El año pasado vendimos más productos que nunca.	Last year we sold more products than ever.
Vendieron la casa en menos de una semana.	They sold the house in less than a week.
Mi primo vendía limonada en la esquina.	My cousin used to sell lemonade on the corner.
Algún día venderé todo y me iré de viaje.	One day I will sell everything and go traveling.
No quiero venderlo, incluso si me ofrecen mucho.	I don't want to sell it, even if they offer me a lot.
Necesito vender estas cosas antes de mudarme.	I need to sell these things before I move.

143 – acordar(se)	**to agree, remember**
Acordamos reunirnos a las cinco de la tarde.	We agreed to meet at five in the afternoon.
El comité acordó posponer la votación.	The committee agreed to postpone the vote.
No lograron acordar el precio.	They couldn't agree on the price.
Acordamos dividirnos el trabajo equitativamente.	We agreed to divide the work equally.
Los países acordaron reducir las emisiones.	The countries agreed to reduce emissions.
¿Te acuerdas de lo que pasó ayer?	Do you remember what happened yesterday?
No me acuerdo dónde dejé mis llaves.	I don't remember where I left my keys.
Él no se acuerda de su contraseña.	He doesn't remember his password.
Nos acordamos de reservar el hotel.	We remembered to book the hotel.
Acuérdate de llamar a tu mamá.	Remember to call your mom.

144 – desear	**to desire, express wish**
Te deseo lo mejor.	I wish you the best.
Le deseamos mucha suerte.	We wish you lots of luck.
¿Desea algo más?	Would you like anything else?
¿Qué deseas para tu cumpleaños?	What would you like for your birthday?
Estoy deseando verte.	I'm looking forward to seeing you.
Deseamos que todo salga bien.	We hope everything goes well.
Siempre deseé visitar Japón.	I always wished to visit Japan.
Cuando era niño, deseaba ser astronauta.	When I was a child, I wished to be an astronaut.
Todos le desearon feliz cumpleaños.	Everyone wished him a happy birthday.
Siempre hemos deseado visitar ese lugar.	We have always wished to visit that place.

145 – iniciar — **to initiate, start**

¿Ya has iniciado el sistema?	Have you already started the system?
Para iniciar el sistema, presiona el botón verde.	To start the system, press the green button.
Se inició una investigación interna.	An internal investigation was initiated.
La empresa inició un proceso de reestructuración.	The company initiated a restructuring process.
Iniciaron una investigación sobre el caso.	They initiated an investigation into the case.
Haz clic aquí para iniciar la descarga.	Click here to initiate the download.
El programa tarda unos segundos en iniciar.	The program takes a few seconds to start.
La empresa decidió iniciar una investigación.	The company decided to start an investigation.
Vamos a iniciar las negociaciones con los sindicatos.	We're going to initiate negotiations with the unions.
Para iniciar el programa, haz doble clic en el ícono.	To start the program, double-click on the icon.

146 – descansar — **to rest**

Mi abuelo descansa después de almorzar.	My grandfather rests after lunch.
Estoy descansando un rato.	I'm resting for a bit.
Descansamos una hora y seguimos.	We rested for an hour and kept going.
No he descansado en todo el día.	I haven't rested all day.
Descansaban bajo la sombra de un árbol.	They were resting under the shade of a tree.
Descansaré después de terminar este proyecto.	I will rest after finishing this project.
Déjalo descansar, ha tenido un día largo.	Let him rest, he's had a long day.
Los atletas necesitan descansar adecuadamente.	Athletes need to rest properly.
Vamos a descansar antes de continuar.	Let's rest before continuing.
Necesito descansar un poco.	I need to rest a little.

147 – observar — **to observe**

Observo a la gente mientras tomo café.	I observe people while I drink coffee.
Los científicos observan las estrellas con telescopios.	Scientists observe the stars with telescopes.
Si observas con atención, verás una diferencia.	If you observe carefully, you'll see a difference.
El científico observó un comportamiento inusual.	The scientist observed unusual behavior.
Observé cómo el gato se movía antes de saltar.	I observed how the cat moved before jumping.
El profesor nos observaba durante el examen.	The teacher observed us during the exam.
Los investigadores observaron a los animales.	The researchers observed the animals.
Me gusta observar a la gente en la plaza.	I like to observe people in the square.
En el experimento, tenían que observar los cambios.	In the experiment, they had to observe the changes.
Desde la ventana se observa el parque.	From the window, one can observe the park.

148 – crecer | **to grow**

Estás creciendo muy rápido, hijo. | You're growing very fast, son.
El árbol crece hacia la luz. | The tree grows toward the light.
Los niños crecen muy rápido. | Children grow very quickly.
Las plantas crecen mejor con suficiente luz solar. | Plants grow better with enough sunlight.
Mi hijo está creciendo sano y fuerte. | My son is growing up healthy and strong.
Mi hija ha crecido mucho este año. | My daughter has grown a lot this year.
¿Dónde creciste? | Where did you grow up?
Crecí en una ciudad pequeña. | I grew up in a small town.
Queremos que la empresa siga creciendo. | We want the company to keep growing.
Déjate crecer la barba este invierno. | Let your beard grow this winter.

149 – elegir | **to elect, choose**

Siempre elijo la opción más saludable. | I always choose the healthiest option.
Eliges siempre los mejores restaurantes. | You always choose the best restaurants.
Él elige con cuidado sus palabras. | He chooses his words carefully.
Nosotros elegimos representantes cada cuatro años. | We elect representatives every four years.
Ella eligió estudiar medicina. | She chose to study medicine.
El pueblo eligió un nuevo presidente. | The people elected a new president.
Elegiremos el mejor candidato para el puesto. | We will choose the best candidate for the position.
Yo de ti, elegiría algo más simple. | If I were you, I'd choose something simpler.
Elegir bien evita arrepentimientos. | Choosing well avoids regrets.
Es difícil elegir entre dos buenas opciones. | It's hard to choose between two good options.

150 – valer | **to be worth**

No vale la pena. | It's not worth it.
Esta casa vale mucho más de lo que pagué. | This house is worth much more than what I paid.
La honestidad vale más que el dinero. | Honesty is worth more than money.
Eso no vale lo que cuesta. | That's not worth what it costs.
Mi casa vale el doble ahora. | My house is worth double now.
Valió la pena esperar. | It was worth the wait.
Esa experiencia valió más que cualquier clase. | That experience was worth more than any class.
El esfuerzo ha valido la pena. | The effort has been worth it.
Valdría la pena intentarlo otra vez. | It would be worth trying again.
Esa inversión valdrá más en cinco años. | That investment will be worth more in five years.

151 – regresar | **to return, come back, go back**

Mañana regreso a casa. | I'm coming back home tomorrow.
Mi hijo regresa de la universidad para Navidad. | My son is returning from university for Christmas.
¿A qué hora regresas a casa? | What time are you coming home?
Me regresé a casa porque olvidé la billetera. | I went back home because I forgot my wallet.
Regresé de Europa después de seis meses. | I returned from Europe after six months.
El dolor regresó después de una semana. | The pain returned after a week.
Nos regresamos cuando empezó a llover. | We went back when it started raining.
El doctor regresará en una hora. | The doctor will be back in an hour.
Me gustaría regresar a ese lugar algún día. | I would like to return to that place someday.
No quiero regresar, me trae malos recuerdos. | I don't want to go back, it brings back bad memories.

152 – significar | **to mean, signify**

¿Qué significa esta palabra? | What does this word mean?
Para mí, la familia significa todo. | For me, family means everything.
No sé qué significa ese símbolo. | I don't know what that symbol means.
Esto significa que tenemos que salir temprano. | This means we have to leave early.
¿Sabes lo que significa esta palabra? | Do you know what this word means?
La victoria significó mucho para el equipo. | The victory meant a lot to the team.
Esa decisión significó el fin del proyecto. | That decision meant the end of the project.
De niño, la Navidad significaba regalos y familia. | As a kid, Christmas meant gifts and family.
Un trabajo nuevo significaría mudarnos a otra ciudad. | A new job would mean moving to another city.
Graduarse significará nuevas oportunidades. | Graduating will mean new opportunities.

153 – interesar | **to interest, be interested**

Me interesa la política. | I'm interested in politics.
Me interesa mucho la historia. | History interests me a lot.
¿Te interesa aprender francés? | Are you interested in learning French?
A los niños les interesa todo. | Children are interested in everything.
Me interesé por la política en la universidad. | I got interested in politics at university.
No nos interesa comprar esa casa. | We're not interested in buying that house.
¿Te interesaría trabajar aquí? | Would you be interested in working here?
Me interesé por la fotografía hace poco. | I recently got interested in photography.
¿Alguna vez te has interesado por aprender japonés? | Have you ever been interested in learning Japanese?
¿No te interesa lo que está pasando? | Don't you care about what's going on?

154 – matar	**to kill**
Mato el tiempo viendo videos en YouTube.	I kill time watching YouTube videos.
El calor me está matando.	The heat is killing me.
Los mosquitos matan al transmitir enfermedades.	Mosquitoes kill by transmitting diseases.
Ese trabajo lo está matando.	That job is killing him.
Mataron al protagonista en la segunda temporada.	They killed the main character in the second season.
Lo mataron en un robo.	They killed him during a robbery.
No matarás.	Thou shalt not kill.
Mataría por una taza de café ahora.	I'd kill for a cup of coffee right now.
No puedes matar una idea tan fácilmente.	You can't kill an idea that easily.
Dicen que matar al mensajero no resuelve nada.	They say killing the messenger doesn't solve anything.

155 – compartir	**to share**
Comparto tu opinión sobre este tema.	I share your opinion on this topic.
Ella siempre comparte sus ideas con el equipo.	She always shares her ideas with the team.
Ellos comparten un apartamento en el centro.	They share an apartment downtown.
Compartí cuarto con mi hermano por años.	I shared a room with my brother for years.
El profesor compartió recursos útiles con la clase.	The teacher shared useful resources with the class.
Compartimos habitación durante toda la universidad.	We shared a room throughout college.
Los hermanos compartieron la herencia por igual.	The siblings shared the inheritance equally.
Hemos compartido muchos momentos juntos.	We have shared many moments together.
Compartiremos los resultados cuando estén listos.	We will share the results when they are ready.
¿Me compartes ese archivo?	Can you share that file with me?

156 – partir	**to leave, depart, split, break**
El autobús parte a las seis en punto.	The bus leaves at 6:00 on the dot.
La expedición parte al amanecer.	The expedition departs at dawn.
Los soldados parten hacia la frontera.	The soldiers depart for the border.
El vuelo partió con dos horas de retraso.	The flight departed two hours late.
Él partió sin despedirse.	He left without saying goodbye.
Se partió la rama.	The branch broke.
Ayer partí temprano para evitar el tráfico.	Yesterday I left early to avoid traffic.
El hielo se partió bajo sus pies.	The ice broke under his feet.
Mis padres partieron a la playa esta mañana.	My parents left for the beach this morning.
¿Puedes partir el pan por la mitad?	Can you break the bread in half?

157 – mandar | **to send, order**

Te mando la foto ahora. | I'll send you the photo now.
¿Quién manda aquí? | Who's in charge here?
Mandamos flores a su casa por su cumpleaños. | We sent flowers to her house for her birthday.
El jefe me mandó terminar el informe hoy. | The boss ordered me to finish the report today.
Mandé arreglar el refrigerador. | I had the refrigerator fixed.
Te mandé un mensaje ayer y no respondiste. | I sent you a message yesterday and you didn't reply.
¿A quién le mandaste ese paquete? | Who did you send that package to?
Mamá me mandó a comprar leche. | Mom sent me to buy milk.
Le mandaron una carta de advertencia. | They sent him a warning letter.
¿Puedes mandarme el enlace otra vez? | Can you send me the link again?

158 – participar | **to participate**

Participo cuando tengo ganas. | I participate when I feel like it.
Si participas más, aprenderás más rápido. | If you participate more, you'll learn faster.
Los niños participan activamente en la clase de arte. | Children participate actively in art class.
Él siempre participaba en los deportes del colegio. | He always took part in school sports.
Mi hijo participó en la obra de teatro del colegio. | My son participated in the school play.
Nunca he participado en carreras, pero me gustaría. | I've never participated in races, but I'd like to.
Participar en estos eventos me hace feliz. | Participating in these events makes me happy.
¿Cuántos equipos van a participar? | How many teams are going to participate?
Quería participar, pero tenía otros compromisos. | I wanted to participate, but I had other commitments.
Buscamos más gente para participar en el proyecto. | We're looking for more people to join the project.

159 – llenar | **to fill**

Me lleno con poca comida. | I get full with little food.
El sótano se llena de agua cuando llueve. | The basement fills with water when it rains.
Llena el salero, está vacío. | Fill the salt shaker, it's empty.
¿Llenamos los globos con agua o con aire? | Are we filling the balloons with water or air?
Se llenó el estadio de gente. | The stadium filled up with people.
Se me llenaron los ojos de lágrimas. | My eyes filled with tears.
Las calles se llenaron de gente por el desfile. | The streets filled with people for the parade.
Tienes que llenar este formulario. | You have to fill out this form.
Necesito llenar mi botella de agua. | I need to fill my water bottle.
Voy a llenar el tanque. | I'm going to fill the tank.

160 – acompañar | **to accompany, go with, keep company**

¿Quieres que te acompañe al médico? | Do you want me to go with you to the doctor?
Mi hermano me acompañó en el viaje. | My brother accompanied me on the trip.
Mi perro me acompaña cuando salgo a correr. | My dog accompanies me when I go running.
El pianista acompañó al cantante en el concierto. | The pianist accompanied the singer at the concert.
La música acompaña perfectamente a la película. | The music perfectly accompanies the movie.
Te puedo acompañar si no quieres ir solo. | I can go with you if you don't want to go alone.
Lo acompañaron en su dolor. | They were there for him in his grief.
Acompañó sus palabras con una sonrisa. | He accompanied his words with a smile.
Freí unas papas para acompañar el pescado. | I fried some potatoes to go with the fish.
El vino blanco acompaña bien los mariscos. | White wine goes well with seafood.

161 – construir | **to build, construct**

Construyo muebles en mi tiempo libre. | I build furniture in my free time.
Están construyendo un puente nuevo. | They are building a new bridge.
Construí una casa con mis propias manos. | I built a house with my own hands.
La empresa ha construido diez edificios este año. | The company has built ten buildings this year.
¿Quién construyó este puente? | Who built this bridge?
Están construyendo un centro comercial. | They are building a shopping mall.
Ella construiría una casa si tuviera dinero. | She would build a house if she had money.
Construirán una carretera nueva. | They will build a new road.
Construir castillos de arena es divertido. | Building sandcastles is fun.
Queremos construir una casa nueva. | We want to build a new house.

162 – enseñar | **to teach, show**

Ella enseña matemáticas en una escuela primaria. | She teaches math at an elementary school.
Él enseña piano. | He teaches piano.
Los buenos profesores enseñan con paciencia. | Good teachers teach with patience.
Mi madre me enseñó a cocinar. | My mother taught me how to cook.
Le están enseñando inglés a su hijo. | They're teaching their son English.
¿Te enseñaron los resultados del examen? | Did they show you the test results?
La vida me ha enseñado a ser paciente. | Life has taught me to be patient.
Me gusta enseñar español a extranjeros. | I enjoy teaching Spanish to foreigners.
Te voy a enseñar a nadar este verano. | I'm going to teach you how to swim this summer.
¿Puedes enseñarme a usar esta aplicación? | Can you teach me to use this app?

163 – parar | **to stop**
Siempre paro en esa tienda camino al trabajo. | I always stop at that store on my way to work.
El autobús para en la esquina. | The bus stops at the corner.
Para el carro aquí, voy a bajar. | Stop the car here, I'm getting out.
No paran de hablar. | They won't stop talking.
Mi reloj se paró cuando murió mi esposa. | My watch stopped when my wife died.
Me paré para saludar a mi vecino. | I stopped to greet my neighbor.
Paró de nevar después de tres horas. | It stopped snowing after three hours.
Paramos a almorzar en un restaurante pequeño. | We stopped to have lunch at a small restaurant.
¿Te has parado a pensar en las consecuencias? | Have you stopped to think about the consequences?
No puedo parar de reír. | I can't stop laughing.

164 – cubrir | **to cover**
Cubre la olla con una tapa. | Cover the pot with a lid.
Las nubes cubren el cielo. | The clouds cover the sky.
Este seguro cubre los gastos médicos. | This insurance covers medical expenses.
Yo cubro a mi jefa cuando está de vacaciones. | I cover for my boss when she's on vacation.
Me cubrí con una manta porque tenía frío. | I covered myself with a blanket because I was cold.
La nieve cubría toda la montaña. | Snow covered the entire mountain.
Al cubrir la herida, evitarás una infección. | By covering the wound, you will avoid an infection.
Cubrieron el cuerpo con una sábana blanca. | They covered the body with a white sheet.
Ellos siempre están cubriendo los errores de su jefe. | They are always covering up their boss's mistakes.
La empresa cubrirá los costos del viaje. | The company will cover the travel costs.

165 – entregar | **to deliver, hand over, submit**
Siempre entrego mi trabajo a tiempo. | I always hand in my work on time.
La compañía entrega pedidos en veinticuatro horas. | The company delivers orders within 24 hours.
¿Ya entregaste la tarea de matemáticas? | Did you turn in the math homework yet?
El cartero entregó el paquete. | The mailman delivered the package.
El paquete fue entregado en la recepción. | The package was delivered to the front desk.
El ladrón se entregó a la policía. | The thief turned himself in to the police.
Entregaremos los premios al final del evento. | We will hand out the awards at the end of the event.
Tengo que entregar el informe antes del viernes. | I have to submit the report before Friday.
Los estudiantes deben entregar la tarea mañana. | Students must hand in homework tomorrow.
Voy a entregar estos documentos al cliente. | I'm going to deliver these documents to the client.

166 – llorar — **to cry**

Siempre lloro cuando corto cebollas. — I always cry when I cut onions.
No llores, todo va a estar bien. — Don't cry, everything will be okay.
Todos los bebés lloran cuando tienen hambre. — All babies cry when they are hungry.
¿Por qué estás llorando? — Why are you crying?
Lloré cuando se murió mi perro. — I cried when my dog died.
Mi hija lloró porque no quería dormir. — My daughter cried because she didn't want to sleep.
Lloraron juntos en el funeral. — They cried together at the funeral.
El niño lloraba porque perdió su juguete. — The boy was crying because he lost his toy.
¿Te hizo llorar esa canción? — Did that song make you cry?
Me hizo llorar de la risa. — He made me cry from laughter.

167 – comentar — **to comment on, mention, talk about, discuss**

Comentamos el partido después de verlo. — We discuss the game after watching it.
Muchas personas comentan sin leer el artículo. — Many people comment without reading the article.
Me comentó que llegaría tarde. — He mentioned to me that he would arrive late.
El profesor comentó los errores del examen. — The teacher commented on the exam mistakes.
Los críticos comentaron bien sobre la película. — The critics spoke well of the movie.
Todos comentamos nuestras escenas favoritas. — We all discussed our favorite scenes.
Ella comentó que la película le pareció aburrida. — She commented that the movie seemed boring to her.
Comentamos las noticias en el almuerzo. — We discussed the news at lunch.
No comenté nada para evitar problemas. — I didn't comment on anything to avoid problems.
Solo quería comentar algo rápido. — I just wanted to mention something quickly.

168 – celebrar — **to celebrate**

Vamos a celebrar su cumpleaños este sábado. — We're going to celebrate his birthday this Saturday.
Celebramos la Navidad en familia. — We celebrate Christmas as a family.
Hoy celebramos nuestro aniversario. — Today we celebrate our anniversary.
Mañana celebran el Día de la Madre. — They're celebrating Mother's Day tomorrow.
Yo celebraba cada pequeña victoria. — I used to celebrate every small victory.
Espero que celebremos pronto. — I hope that we celebrate soon.
El festival se celebra cada año. — The festival is celebrated every year.
Ya habían celebrado cuando llegamos. — They had already celebrated when we arrived.
El evento se celebrará en el auditorio principal. — The event will be held in the main auditorium.
El equipo celebró la victoria con entusiasmo. — The team celebrated the victory enthusiastically.

169 – molestar	**to bother**
¿Molesto a alguien si me siento aquí?	Am I bothering anyone if I sit here?
Me molesta que no me escuches.	It bothers me that you don't listen to me.
¿Te molesta si abro la ventana?	Does it bother you if I open the window?
Me molesta cuando la gente habla durante la película.	It bothers me when people talk during the movie.
¡No me molestes ahora!	Don't bother me right now!
Me molesta mucho.	It really bothers me.
Mis vecinos me molestan con su música.	My neighbors bother me with their music.
¿Te molestó lo que dije?	Did what I said bother you?
¡Deja de molestar a tu hermana!	Stop bothering your sister!
No quiero molestarte mientras trabajas.	I don't want to bother you while you work.

170 – aumentar	**to increase**
El gobierno aumenta los impuestos.	The government increases taxes.
Los precios aumentaron un cinco por ciento.	Prices increased by 5%.
Necesitamos aumentar nuestras ventas.	We need to increase our sales.
El precio del petróleo aumentó un diez por ciento.	The price of oil increased by 10%.
La población ha aumentado rápidamente.	The population has increased quickly.
El consumo de energía aumenta durante el verano.	Energy consumption increases during the summer.
Los médicos aumentaron la dosis del medicamento.	The doctors increased the medication dosage.
La población aumentará en los próximos años.	The population will increase in the coming years.
Las ventas aumentarían con una mejor publicidad.	Sales would increase with better advertising.
La demanda por este producto sigue aumentando.	The demand for this product keeps increasing.

171 – casarse	**to get married**
Me caso en junio del próximo año.	I'm getting married in June next year.
Mi hermana se casa con su novio.	My sister is marrying her boyfriend.
Se casaron en una playa al atardecer.	They got married on a beach at sunset.
¿Te casas por amor o por conveniencia?	Are you getting married for love or convenience?
Nos casamos el próximo mes.	We're getting married next month.
Se casaría contigo si se lo pidieras.	She would marry you if you asked her.
Me casé muy joven.	I got married very young.
Se casaron en una ceremonia pequeña.	They got married in a small ceremony.
Aún no he decidido si quiero casarme.	I still haven't decided if I want to get married.
Decidieron casarse después de cinco años juntos.	They decided to get married after five years together.

172 – dañar	**to damage, harm**
Fumar daña los pulmones.	Smoking harms the lungs.
La contaminación daña el medio ambiente.	Pollution harms the environment.
Estos productos dañan la capa de ozono.	These products damage the ozone layer.
El agua dañó mi celular.	The water damaged my phone.
La tormenta dañó el techo de mi casa.	The storm damaged the roof of my house.
Él dijo algo que dañó su imagen pública.	He said something that damaged his public image.
El escándalo dañó su reputación.	The scandal harmed his reputation.
El incendio dañó varios edificios.	The fire damaged several buildings.
Los vándalos dañaron el monumento.	The vandals damaged the monument.
El exceso de sol puede dañar tu piel.	Excess sun can damage your skin.

173 – obligar	**to oblige, force, make, compel**
Mi mamá me obliga a hacer la tarea primero.	My mom makes me do homework first.
Mi conciencia me obliga a decir la verdad.	My conscience compels me to tell the truth.
El contrato me obliga a quedarme otros seis meses.	The contract obliges me to stay another six months.
El mal tiempo nos obligó a cambiar los planes.	The bad weather forced us to change our plans.
La lluvia nos obligó a cancelar el picnic.	The rain forced us to cancel the picnic.
El accidente los obligó a tomar un desvío.	The accident forced them to take a detour.
Mis padres me obligaban a ir a misa.	My parents used to make me go to Mass.
Sus padres la obligaron a estudiar medicina.	Her parents forced her to study medicine.
La situación nos ha obligado a decidir.	The situation has forced us to decide.
No te obligaré a venir si no quieres.	I won't force you to come if you don't want to.

174 – apoyar	**to support**
Apoyo a mi hermana en sus decisiones.	I support my sister in her decisions.
Necesito a alguien que me apoye emocionalmente.	I need someone to support me emotionally.
Apoyamos a la comunidad local con donaciones.	We support the local community with donations.
Apoyan la iniciativa ambiental.	They support the environmental initiative.
Apoyaste a tu amigo cuando más lo necesitaba.	You supported your friend when he needed it most.
Apoyaron nuestra decisión de mudarnos.	They supported our decision to move.
Espero que me apoyes en esta situación difícil.	I hope that you support me in this difficult situation.
Siempre apoyaré a mis amigos en momentos difíciles.	I will always support my friends in difficult times.
Él apoyará a su equipo en el partido de mañana.	He will support his team in tomorrow's game.
No debemos apoyar decisiones injustas.	We shouldn't support unfair decisions.

175 – quitar | **to take off, remove, take away**

Me quito los zapatos al entrar a casa. — I take off my shoes when I get home.
Le quito las llaves del carro cuando bebe. — I take away his car keys when he drinks.
Esta mancha no se quita con agua. — This stain doesn't come out with water.
Le quito el celular si no hace la tarea. — I take his phone away if he doesn't do his homework.
El profesor le quitó el teléfono al estudiante. — The teacher took the phone away from the student.
Me quité el abrigo porque hacía calor adentro. — I took off my coat because it was warm inside.
El doctor me quitó los puntos ayer. — The doctor removed my stitches yesterday.
No me he quitado estos zapatos en todo el día. — I haven't taken off these shoes all day.
Pronto me quitarán los brackets. — They'll remove my braces soon.
Tengo que quitar esta mancha de la camisa. — I have to remove this stain from the shirt.

176 – contestar | **to answer, reply**

Contesto todos mis correos cada mañana. — I answer all my emails every morning.
¿Por qué no contestas el teléfono? — Why aren't you answering the phone?
No contesté porque no reconocí el número. — I didn't answer because I didn't recognize the number.
Ella nunca contesta mis mensajes de texto. — She never answers my text messages.
El estudiante contestó todo bien. — The student answered everything correctly.
Nadie contestó cuando toqué el timbre. — Nobody answered when I rang the doorbell.
Contesté todas las preguntas del examen. — I answered all the questions on the test.
Le contestamos al profesor con una pregunta. — We replied to the teacher with a question.
Estoy esperando que me contesten. — I'm waiting for them to reply to me.
Contestaré cuando tenga tiempo. — I'll reply when I have time.

177 – prender | **to turn on, light, ignite, catch fire**

El carro no prende. — The car won't start.
Prende la tele. — Turn on the TV.
Ya prendí el carro. — I already started the car.
El techo se prendió en llamas después del rayo. — The roof caught fire after the lightning strike.
Se prendió solo. — It turned on by itself.
Prendimos la fogata en la playa. — We lit the bonfire on the beach.
Se me olvidó prender la estufa. — I forgot to turn on the stove.
No puedo prender la moto. — I can't start the motorcycle.
No puedo prender mi celular, murió la batería. — I can't turn on my phone, the battery died.
¿Puedes prender la luz? — Can you turn on the light?

178 – depender	**to depend**
Dependo de mi mujer como apoyo financiero.	I depend on my wife for financial support.
Todo depende de ti.	Everything depends on you.
Depende de las circunstancias.	It depends on the circumstances.
Dependemos completamente de la tecnología.	We completely depend on technology.
¿Vas a ir? Depende.	Will you go? It depends.
Dependí de mis amigos cuando estuve enfermo.	I depended on my friends when I was sick.
Él siempre ha dependido de su familia.	He has always depended on his family.
Mi decisión dependerá de varios factores.	My decision will depend on various factors.
Antes dependía mucho de los demás, pero ya no.	I used to depend a lot on others, but not anymore.
No quiero depender de nadie.	I don't want to depend on anyone.

179 – acostar	**to put to bed, lie down, go to bed**
¿A qué hora acuestas normalmente a tu bebé?	At what time do you normally put your baby to bed?
Acuesto a los niños a las siete.	I put the kids to bed at seven.
Me voy a acostar, estoy agotado.	I'm going to bed, I'm exhausted.
Ella acostó al bebé con cuidado.	She gently put the baby to bed.
Se acostó y se quedó dormido enseguida.	He lay down and fell asleep right away.
¿Ya se acostaron los niños?	Have the kids gone to bed yet?
Vamos a acostarnos temprano para madrugar mañana.	Let's go to bed early to wake up early tomorrow.
En verano me acuesto más tarde que en invierno.	In summer I go to bed later than in winter.
Me acuesto temprano durante la semana.	I go to bed early during the week.
El médico me recomendó acostarme boca arriba.	The doctor recommended that I lie on my back.

180 – reír	**to laugh**
Me río cada vez que veo ese video.	I laugh every time I see that video.
¿De qué te ríes?	What are you laughing at?
Ella se ríe con muchas ganas cuando ve esa película.	She laughs out loud when she watches that movie.
Cuando estoy con ellos, siempre me estoy riendo.	When I'm with them, I'm always laughing.
Nos reímos tanto que casi no podíamos respirar.	We laughed so much we could barely breathe.
Nunca me he reído tanto como hoy.	I have never laughed as much as today.
De niños, nos reíamos por cualquier tontería.	As kids, we used to laugh at silly things.
Es bueno reír de vez en cuando.	It's good to laugh once in a while.
Esa película me hace reír.	That movie makes me laugh.
Te vas a reír cuando escuches lo que pasó.	You're going to laugh when you hear what happened.

181 – tirar | **to throw, throw away, pull**

¿Dónde tiro esta botella vacía? | Where do I throw away this empty bottle?
Tira la basura antes de que se llene el basurero. | Throw out the trash before the trash can fills up.
No tires eso, todavía sirve. | Don't throw that away, it still works.
Los niños tiran piedras al río. | The children throw stones into the river.
Estás tirando dinero en esa lotería. | You're wasting money on that lottery.
Mi hermano me tiró una almohada. | My brother threw a pillow at me.
Tiraron monedas a la fuente para pedir un deseo. | They threw coins into the fountain to make a wish.
Tienes que tirar de la cuerda para abrir la cortina. | You have to pull the cord to open the curtain.
Tira de la cuerda con ambas manos. | Pull the rope with both hands.
Tira la pelota justo al centro del blanco. | Throw the ball right at the center of the target.

182 – guardar | **to keep, put away, save**

Siempre guardo las llaves en el mismo lugar. | I always keep the keys in the same place.
Siempre guardo las facturas por si acaso. | I always keep the receipts just in case.
Guarda tus zapatos en el armario. | Put your shoes away in the closet.
¿Dónde guardas tus documentos importantes? | Where do you keep your important documents?
Guardé el abrigo en el perchero. | I put the coat away on the rack.
No te olvides de guardar el documento. | Don't forget to save the document.
Se guardó automáticamente. | It was saved automatically.
Ella guardó silencio durante la reunión. | She kept silent during the meeting.
¿Puedes guardar un secreto? | Can you keep a secret?
Guarda un pedazo de pastel para mí. | Save a piece of cake for me.

183 – gritar | **to yell, shout, scream**

¡No me grites! | Don't yell at me!
Mi madre siempre grita cuando ve una araña. | My mother always screams when she sees a spider.
Los niños gritan de emoción. | The children scream with excitement.
¿Por qué estás gritando? | Why are you shouting?
Mis vecinos se gritan al discutir. | My neighbors yell at each other when they argue.
El entrenador grita instrucciones desde la banda. | The coach shouts instructions from the sideline.
Los fanáticos gritaban emocionados. | The fans were screaming excitedly.
El niño gritó "feliz cumpleaños" muy fuerte. | The child shouted "happy birthday" very loudly.
Gritar no resuelve los problemas. | Yelling doesn't solve problems.
No es necesario gritar, te escucho bien. | No need to shout, I can hear you fine.

184 – despertar | **to wake up**

Despierto a mis hijos a las siete de la mañana.	I wake my kids up at seven in the morning.
El ruido despertó al bebé.	The noise woke the baby.
Despierto a mis hijos con abrazos y besos.	I wake my kids with hugs and kisses.
Los padres despertaron a sus hijos para ir al colegio.	The parents woke their children up to go to school.
Me despierto temprano para despertar a los demás.	I wake up early to wake up the others.
Me despierto todos los días a las seis y media.	I wake up every day at 6:30.
Me desperté por un ruido.	I woke up because of a noise.
Los niños se despiertan temprano los fines de semana.	The children wake up early on weekends.
¿A qué hora te despertaste esta mañana?	What time did you wake up this morning?
Siempre me cuesta despertarme temprano.	I always have a hard time waking up early.

185 – amar | **to love**

Siempre te voy a amar, pase lo que pase.	I will always love you, no matter what happens.
Amar es dar sin esperar nada.	To love is to give without expecting anything.
Amar a quien no se ama es difícil.	Loving someone who doesn't love themselves is hard.
Ella ama a sus hijos con todo el corazón.	She loves her children with all her heart.
María ha amado la música clásica desde que era niña.	Maria has loved classical music since she was a child.
¿Has amado alguna vez de verdad?	Have you ever truly loved?
Amamos la libertad y luchamos por ella.	We love freedom and fight for it.
Si amas a alguien, debes respetar su libertad.	If you love someone, you must respect their freedom.
Mi abuela amó a mi abuelo hasta el final.	My grandmother loved my grandfather until the end.
Ellos se han amado por más de cincuenta años.	They have loved each other for over fifty years.

186 – vestirse | **to get dressed**

Me visto justo después de despertarme.	I get dressed right after I wake up.
Te vistes muy bien.	You dress very well.
Los niños se visten solos a partir de los cuatro años.	Children dress themselves starting at age four.
Me vestí rápido porque iba tarde.	I got dressed quickly because I was running late.
¿Ya te vestiste para la fiesta?	Did you already get dressed for the party?
Él se vistió de negro para el funeral.	He dressed in black for the funeral.
Ya me he vestido, solo falta peinarme.	I've already gotten dressed, I just need to do my hair.
Ella se vestía muy formal para el trabajo.	She used to dress very formally for work.
Me vestiré en cuanto termine de ducharme.	I'll get dressed as soon as I finish showering.
Los niños no saben vestirse solos.	The children don't know how to dress themselves.

187 – enviar

to send

Te envío el archivo.
I'm sending you the file.

¿Me envías la información?
Are you sending me the information?

Envíale mis saludos a tu hermana.
Send my regards to your sister.

Envié las invitaciones ayer.
I sent the invitations yesterday.

¿A quién le enviaste flores?
Who did you send flowers to?

Ellos enviaron sus currículums a varias empresas.
They sent their résumés to several companies.

¿Por qué no lo has enviado todavía?
Why haven't you sent it yet?

El jefe me pidió que enviara el informe hoy.
The boss asked me to send the report today.

Te enviaré la información por correo electrónico.
I'll send you the information by email.

Voy a enviar un correo ahora mismo.
I'm going to send an email right now.

188 – lavar

to wash

Me lavo las manos antes de comer.
I wash my hands before eating.

Lavo la ropa los fines de semana.
I wash the clothes on weekends.

¿Te lavas el pelo todos los días?
Do you wash your hair every day?

Ella se lava el pelo cada dos días.
She washes her hair every other day.

Lavamos el carro solo dos veces al año.
We wash our car only twice per year.

Nos lavamos las manos con jabón antibacterial.
We wash our hands with antibacterial soap.

Ella se lava la cara cuando se despierta.
She washes her face when she wakes up.

Ella se lavó la herida con agua limpia.
She washed the wound with clean water.

Lavaré toda la ropa después de nuestras vacaciones.
I will wash all the clothes after our vacation.

¿Podrías lavar los platos sucios, por favor?
Would you wash the dirty dishes, please?

189 – preferir

to prefer

¿Prefieres café o té?
Do you prefer coffee or tea?

Prefiero el café sin azúcar.
I prefer coffee without sugar.

Los niños prefieren jugar videojuegos.
The children prefer playing video games.

Preferimos caminar en lugar de tomar el autobús.
We prefer to walk instead of taking the bus.

Preferí quedarme en casa porque llovía mucho.
I preferred to stay home because it was raining hard.

Él prefirió quedarse con sus amigos.
He preferred to stay with his friends.

Prefirieron no viajar durante la pandemia.
They preferred not to travel during the pandemic.

Cuando era niño, prefería los dulces a las verduras.
When I was a child, I preferred candy to vegetables.

Siempre hemos preferido calidad sobre cantidad.
We've always preferred quality over quantity.

Yo preferiría trabajar desde casa si es posible.
I would prefer to work from home if possible.

190 – cantar	**to sing**
Canto en la ducha.	I sing in the shower.
Cantas muy bien.	You sing very well.
Ella canta en un coro.	She sings in a choir.
Cantan en varios idiomas.	They sing in various languages.
Yo cantaría si no fuera tan tímido.	I would sing if I weren't so shy.
He cantado esta canción mil veces.	I have sung this song a thousand times.
Ellos cantaron el himno nacional.	They sang the national anthem.
Siempre cantábamos juntos cuando éramos niños.	We always used to sing together when we were kids.
Cantaremos villancicos en Navidad.	We will sing Christmas carols at Christmas.
A ella le encanta cantar en la ducha.	She loves singing in the shower.

191 – producir	**to produce**
La empresa produce autos eléctricos.	The company produces electric cars.
Los agricultores producen más frutas en verano.	Farmers produce more fruit in summer.
Ese queso se produce solo en esta región.	That cheese is only produced in this region.
El cuerpo produce serotonina cuando haces ejercicio.	The body produces serotonin when you exercise.
Antes mi jardín producía muchos tomates.	My garden used to produce many tomatoes before.
Este año hemos producido más que nunca.	This year we have produced more than ever.
La empresa ha producido más contenido digital.	The company has produced more digital content.
Nunca habían producido algo tan complejo.	They had never produced something so complex.
Este año produciremos el doble que el pasado.	This year we will produce twice as much as last year.
La nueva planta producirá energía limpia.	The new plant will produce clean energy.

192 – considerar	**to consider, regard**
Lo considero un buen amigo.	I consider him a good friend.
Considero que este es el mejor restaurante.	I consider this the best restaurant.
¿Te consideras una persona creativa?	Do you consider yourself a creative person?
Ella considera que es una buena oportunidad.	She considers it a good opportunity.
Mucha gente lo consideran un genio.	Many people consider him a genius.
El juez consideró todas las pruebas.	The judge considered all the evidence.
Consideramos esa opción, pero la descartamos.	We considered that option but ruled it out.
Considera los pros y los contras antes de decidir.	Consider the pros and cons before deciding.
Los expertos consideran que es un gran avance.	Experts regard it as a great advancement.
Debes considerar todas las opciones antes de decidir.	You should consider all options before deciding.

193 – utilizar | **to utilize, use**

¿Qué programa utilizas para editar tus videos? | What program do you use to edit your videos?
En el hospital utilizan equipos de última generación. | At the hospital they use state-of-the-art equipment.
Utilizamos protocolos estrictos en la fábrica. | We use strict protocols at the factory.
Se está utilizando demasiada energía en esta planta. | Too much energy is being used in this plant.
El doctor utilizó un nuevo procedimiento. | The doctor used a new procedure.
Utilizamos mapas antiguos para encontrar el tesoro. | We used old maps to find the treasure.
Mi abuela utilizaba remedios caseros para todo. | My grandmother used home remedies for everything.
¿Alguna vez has utilizado este tipo de herramienta? | Have you ever used this type of tool?
Los arquitectos utilizarán materiales sostenibles. | The architects will use sustainable materials.
Deberías aprender a utilizar mejor tu tiempo libre. | You should learn to use your free time better.

194 – cortar | **to cut**

El cuchillo no corta bien. | The knife doesn't cut well.
El carnicero corta la carne con mucha precisión. | The butcher cuts the meat with great precision.
Me corté el dedo con el cuchillo. | I cut my finger with the knife.
El peluquero me cortó el pelo demasiado corto. | The hairdresser cut my hair too short.
La llamada se cortó. | The call got cut off.
Él ha cortado todos los lazos con su familia. | He has cut all ties with his family.
Cortamos el pastel y lo repartimos. | We cut the cake and shared it.
Él siempre me corta cuando estoy hablando. | He always cuts me off when I'm talking.
Ten cuidado de no cortarte con el cuchillo. | Be careful not to cut yourself with the knife.
Corta las verduras en trozos pequeños. | Cut the vegetables into small pieces.

195 – gastar | **to spend**

Él gasta demasiado en salir a comer. | He spends too much on eating out.
Gastamos mucho en comida. | We spend a lot on food.
Gasté mucho dinero. | I spent a lot of money.
¿Cuánto gastaste? | How much did you spend?
Gasté cien euros en ropa. | I spent a hundred euros on clothes.
Ya gasté toda mi mesada. | I already spent my whole allowance.
Gastamos todos nuestros ahorros en esta casa. | We spent all our savings on this house.
¿En qué gastarás tu bono de Navidad? | What will you spend your Christmas bonus on?
No deberías gastar tanto en videojuegos. | You shouldn't spend so much on video games.
¿Cuánto has gastado en estas vacaciones? | How much have you spent on this vacation?

196 – soler | **to usually do, tend to do**

Suelo levantarme temprano los fines de semana. | I usually wake up early on weekends.
Suelo desayunar a las siete. | I usually have breakfast at seven.
Aquí suele hacer mucho calor en verano. | It's usually very hot here in summer.
Mi mamá suele llamarme los domingos. | My mom usually calls me on Sundays.
Los niños suelen jugar en el parque. | The children usually play in the park.
Solemos cenar juntos los viernes. | We usually eat dinner together on Fridays.
No solemos ver televisión durante la semana. | We don't usually watch TV during the week.
Yo solía caminar al trabajo cuando vivía más cerca. | I used to walk to work when I lived closer.
De niño, solía jugar fútbol con mis amigos. | As a child, I used to play soccer with my friends.
Solíamos ir al cine todos los viernes por la noche. | We used to go to the movies every Friday night.

197 – apagar | **to turn off, put out**

Apaga la luz antes de salir. | Turn off the light before leaving.
Olvidé apagar el horno. | I forgot to turn off the oven.
Apagué el televisor porque nadie lo estaba viendo. | I turned off the TV because no one was watching it.
Los guardias apagan las luces a medianoche. | The guards turn off the lights at midnight.
Siempre apago la computadora al terminar de trabajar. | I always turn off the computer when I finish working.
Apagamos el fuego con arena y agua. | We put out the fire with sand and water.
Los bomberos apagaron el incendio rápidamente. | The firefighters quickly put out the fire.
¿Por qué se apagó la pantalla? | Why did the screen turn off?
Antes, apagaban las velas para dormir. | They used to put out the candles before sleeping.
La hoguera está apagándose lentamente. | The bonfire is slowly dying out.

198 – funcionar | **to function, work**

La página web no funciona en mi celular. | The website doesn't work on my phone.
El aire acondicionado no funciona. | The air conditioning doesn't work.
La computadora no funciona. | The computer isn't working.
¿Por qué no funciona? | Why doesn't it work?
Si no funciona, prueba otra cosa. | If it doesn't work, try something else.
Este programa funciona en todos los sistemas. | This program works on all systems.
Este método funciona bien para aprender idiomas. | This method works well for learning languages.
El plan no funcionó como esperábamos. | The plan didn't work as we expected.
El plan funcionó mejor de lo esperado. | The plan worked better than expected.
Eso no va a funcionar. | That's not going to work.

199 – mentir — **to lie**

Yo nunca miento.	I never lie.
¿Por qué mienten tanto los políticos?	Why do politicians lie so much?
Los niños a veces mienten.	Children sometimes lie.
No entiendo por qué me mentirías.	I don't understand why you would lie to me.
Te mentí, lo siento.	I lied to you, I'm sorry.
Sé que me estás mintiendo.	I know you're lying to me.
¿Por qué mentiste sobre eso?	Why did you lie about that?
Ella te mintió en la cara.	She lied to your face.
Le mentí a mi mamá.	I lied to my mom.
Es fácil mentir, pero difícil sostener la mentira.	It's easy to lie, but hard to maintain the lie.

200 – mudar — **to move (to a new place)**

Me mudo cada pocos años por mi trabajo.	I move every few years for my job.
Mi hermana se muda a Barcelona por trabajo.	My sister is moving to Barcelona for work.
Me mudé por trabajo.	I moved because of work.
¿Ya te mudaste o sigues ahí?	Did you move already or are you still there?
Nos mudamos a una casa más grande el mes pasado.	We moved to a bigger house last month.
Mis padres se mudaron a otra ciudad cuando era niño.	My parents moved to another city when I was a child.
Nos hemos mudado tres veces en cinco años.	We've moved three times in five years.
Se mudarán la próxima semana.	They'll move next week.
Estoy pensando en mudarme más cerca del trabajo.	I'm thinking of moving closer to work.
No quiero mudarme, me encanta este barrio.	I don't want to move, I love this neighborhood.

www.ingramcontent.com/pod-product-compliance
Lightning Source LLC
LaVergne TN
LVHW080316110826
845155LV00023B/129

* 9 7 8 1 9 5 2 1 6 1 1 3 1 *